Praise for
Beginner with a Black Belt

"Ana's book guides the reader about the importance of the practice, dedication and art behind martial arts and how the many skills and disciplines needed to master life go beyond more than just martial arts. The Author cleverly outlines how her newfound skills on the pathway to her blackbelt have benefitted her in her everyday life and shows readers the importance of understanding how vital these skills have been in furthering her professional and personal life. A new take on an old art form."

—Peggy McColl,
New York Times best-selling Author
http://PeggyMcColl.com

"I was so blessed to have Ana Stevanović in the very first workshop I ever gave. She was a wonderful teacher then and she's a wonderful teacher now. In this concise, illuminating book, she guides us through her own inspiring journey that combines the ancient Japanese martial art of Bujinkan with personal development. It's a combination you don't often find which makes this book so special."

—Pam Grout,
#1 New York Times best-selling Author of
*E-Squared, Thank and Grow Rich,
the Course in Miracles Experiment* and 17 other books

"Ana Stevanovic's journey in life, proves that ten two letter words can be your own personal roadmap. " If it is to be, it is up to me". Congratulations as you help people navigate their true potential."

—David Grodski,
best-selling Author of
The Wisdom of Wellness (WOW).

"*Beginner with a Black Belt* is a wonderful book that I enjoyed reading very much. It offers a wonderful blend of personal experiences, and life principles. The parallel between self-development and martial arts practices gives it a very unique and refreshing perspective. I loved Ana's approach to help people improving their lives! An absolute must-read if you are ready to change your habits and better your life."

—Gisele Maxwell,
International best-selling Author of
Free and Rich Beyond Wealthy

Beginner

WITH A BLACK BELT

Become the Master of Your Life Journey

Ana Stevanović

Hasmark PUBLISHING INTERNATIONAL

Published by
Hasmark Publishing International
www.hasmarkpublishing.com

Disclaimer

Permission should be addressed in writing to Ana Stevanović at
ance018@gmail.com

Editor: Judith Scott judith@hasmarkpublishing.com
Book Design: Anne Karklins anne@hasmarkpublishing.com

ISBN 13: 978-1-989756-58-4
ISBN 10: 1989756581

Acknowledgements

This book would not have seen the light of the day without the help of dozens of individuals. I cannot name them all here, but know this: to each and every one of you who I had the honor of meeting and sharing my time with—*thank you*. I have become the person I am today because we crossed paths, and because you selflessly shared with me your wisdom, love, and passion for life.

I am forever grateful to my mom and my dad. Only when we grow into adults ourselves do we truly understand the value of our parents and realize the depth of their sacrifice—a sacrifice that can only be explained by the unconditional love of parents for their children. Both of my parents ingrained in me fundamental human values and they sacrificed everything they could so that I could grow up safe, have a good education, and build my life and career abroad. I am also thankful to Ivan, my brother and best friend, whom I always looked up to and who has fully supported me every single day for more than thirty years. Many thanks to my best friends, Jovana and Milena, for the love they have given me along the way; they included me as integral parts of their families, and they kept our friendships close for decades despite the distances between us.

I want to thank one of my first teachers, Igor Djordjević, who helped me to develop both as a martial artist and as a human. I thank my *sensei* and teacher, Dai Shihan Phil Bradshaw, for opening the doors of his dojo to me after moving to Switzerland and for continuing to guide me on the path of *Bujinkan*. Thanks to Dai Shihan Phillip Legare for providing mentorship throughout my recent growth, as well as during the writing of this book. Special gratitude goes out to Dai Shihan Sveneric Bogsäter; I will never forget you paying for my seminar fee in the days when I had no money to train. Thanks also to Bujinkan Dai Shihan Jack Hoban for his guidance on this book.

I want to thank my university professor, Dr. Goran Tošić, who mentored me while studying dentistry and whom to this day gives me valuable guidance in many areas of my life (including this book). Thanks to the late Professor Biljana Vujičić for showing me how far women can go as doctors and for giving me my first job as a dentist. Thanks to Ueli Breitschmid, CEO and owner of Curaden, for always having his door open to everyone who worked for him. During the years we worked together, he taught me to always ask the right questions and showed me how far passion, vision, and hard work can get you in life.

I want to thank my first coach, Jen Barna, for guiding me through the wonderful world of *Thinking Into Results*, and for enriching my life in so many ways. I am grateful to Pam Grout, a New York Times bestselling author, who fully supported me in my writing and gave me valuable guidance along the way on my path of growth. I am also thankful to New York Times bestselling author, Peggy McColl, for the help she provided on my book-writing journey.

Finally, I want to express my utmost gratitude to the two men who have shaped my life as I know it: Mr. Bob Proctor and Dr.

Masaaki Hatsumi. These two men, each different in their own ways but yet similar in others, have helped me to live a purposeful and valuable life in every sense of the words. As mentors to thousands of people, they help to make this world a worthy place to live. I strive to lead a purposeful life because you both show the way.

Table of Contents

Why Do You Need a Black Belt in Your Life?............xiii

Three Questions..xix

The Principles of Heaven 1

Chapter I – Values 3

Chapter II – Vision 9

Chapter III – Willingness.............................16

Chapter IV – Failure 22

The Principles of Earth...........................27

Chapter V – Space 29

Chapter VI – Paradigms................................33

Chapter VII – Control.................................40

Chapter VIII – Experience.............................45

The Principles of Human 51

Chapter IX – Perseverance.............................53

Chapter X – Weapons 58

Chapter XI – Attitude 66

Chapter XII – Vital Points 71

The Final Chapter - Immovable Spirit 75

In the End 80

Ninjutsu Poem 83

Sources Mentioned in the Book and Further
    Recommendations 84

About the Author 87

Foreword

I've known Ana for several years now as a fellow student of the same martial art, Bujinkan Budo Taijutsu. We met in person in Japan at our Hombu dojo in 2019, where I had the honor of giving her the Sakki test. For martial arts practitioners who are unfamiliar with the Bujinkan's Sakki test, it can be described as the result of a non-physical connection between the giver and receiver. It is a requirement for the rank of Godan (5th degree black belt) and more importantly it is required for the title of Shidoshi (licensed instructor). Ana describes the test quite well in Chapter X Weapons, *Intuition*. Drawing on her own experiences gained from taking the test in the Hombu dojo in front of Hatsumi Sōke and one hundred (plus) students, Ana provides the reader with much valuable insight into the gift of intuition, something we all have, "…that serves to protect our own interest and wellbeing."

What appeals to me most about this book is that Ana writes it from her own personal experiences in overcoming tremendous challenges throughout her life. She guides us through a culmination of life lessons learned from her extensive background in martial arts and her work as a personal development coach. She puts the reader on their own path to self-mastery using the Japanese martial arts concepts of Heaven-Earth-Human (Ten-Chi-Jin), and how Humans are the connection between Heaven and Earth. One might consider this a parallel to western psychology's concept of Thought-Word-Deed, with the Deed being the connection, or end result of Thought and Word. In my Sentinel International, Personal Protective Measures training programs, we use a similar training mantra known as: Assess-Plan-Act. These mantras can be used as a framework to achieving our own self-mastery.

Anyone seeking to better themselves will get a lot out of reading this book. It provides you the necessary framework to put you on the path of self-discovery and enlightenment. It is heavily referenced with useful quotes and books from progressive thinkers throughout history that will trigger many "ah ha" moments and pauses for self-reflection. This book will also resonate well with martial arts practitioners, especially those in the Bujinkan, with many references to Hatsumi Sōke, Ten-Chi-Jin, and the Sakki test.

I am proud of Ana for having the courage to write her first book, and I hope many more will follow. When you read it, you will understand that she bared her soul in writing it. Her doing so makes it much easier for us to bare our own souls, if only to ourselves.

Dai Shihan Phillip Legare (15. Dan) is a senior student in the Bujinkan, Head of the Bujinkan Taka Seigi Dojo, and Founder of Sentinel International. He is a retired Marine Combat Veteran and also retired Department of Defense Special Agent and senior government official. He lived in Japan off and on for many years throughout both of his previous careers. He can now be found in Hawaii where he teaches martial arts and protection training and is a real estate agent.

Why Do You Need a Black Belt in Your Life?

Success is not final, failure is not fatal: it is the courage to continue that counts.

—Sir Winston Churchill

When asking my sensei what is the purpose of practicing martial arts, he would always reply, "To live." When asking my mentor what is the purpose of having goals, he would always reply, "To grow." And, when asking my teacher what was the reason for many decisions he made in life, he would reply, "To enjoy." Each had a different approach to life, yet they all agreed on one thing: life is all about growing on your path and enjoying each step along the way.

As every good student would, I did my best to listen carefully and to grasp everything I was taught. I began practicing martial arts in my teens. I would come home from training with bruises at least three times each week, and I was usually the only girl there—but quitting never crossed my mind. My initial motivation was self-protection. Even though I suffered injuries and ended up in the emergency room at least once, I always came back to the dojo. Although I initially went to learn self-defense, I continued to train because my sensei was teaching me something much more important. He was teaching me how to be a good human being and how to live a purposeful life.

And living a purposeful life was not easy. When I was five years old, our country was hit by a massive economic crisis. War came to our country when I was twelve. Family life was sometimes tough. I was a good student in school, but I struggled in many other ways. Unlike other kids, I loved going to school because it provided stability. I knew exactly how to behave and follow the rules of the game: attend class, study, learn, and pass exams. I cracked that code early in life, and in school I felt as comfortable as a fish in the sea. But outside of school was an entirely different story. Even in stable countries life can often be unpredictable. But in a country that falls apart from one day to the other—where all the values are turned upside down within months, where even the most normal hopes of going to work and having a stable income are gone—that was the code I could not crack.

I thought everything would be different after moving to a more stable environment. After my own experiences I thought the lives of the people living here should be different. Yet very soon I came to realize that the people around me also struggle. I came to understand that even in stable environments people are still programmed to live their life without much thinking: finish school, find a job, begin your career, start a family, and so on. But then, unless it didn't happen already, you start seeing that your planned movie starts having twists and turns.

Maybe you are unhappy in your marriage, or maybe you will get divorced. Maybe you've been fired from your job, or maybe you feel miserable doing it. Maybe your parents died too early.

Or, maybe you have it all but still feel empty and stuck. No one actually tells you that the scenarios we have come to expect can go so wrong. However, they mostly do.

This was the case in my life. Not including the wars, poverty, and instability of my childhood, my first moment of being stuck—and there were several—happened after graduating from dentistry school. Two years into the dental practice I found myself deeply unhappy with my job. I was petrified. It took me six years to earn my license, and I was great at my job. *What the heck should I do now?* I was always taught that whenever I felt stuck, I should go back to basics. In martial arts training, that would mean repeating some fundamental movements. But I didn't know how to go back to basics in my everyday life. I continued telling myself that success isn't final, and failure isn't fatal, and I kept going. I trained.

Training was on and off for me, but I would always come back. Throughout my life of moving to different countries and changing not only my environment, changing the people around me, and changing languages, training was one of two constants that kept me balanced and moving forward.

The other constant was studying philosophies of success from western authors. I was in my early twenties when I first came across the movie *The Secret*. Among several different actors in this movie, one stood out; an old man in a funny suit explained some valuable ideas in a way I really liked.[1] I began to study these topics with the purpose of providing myself with a better and more secure life, and to protect my future and the future of my loved ones from the bad economic, political, and social circumstances that were a daily reality in my childhood.

---

[1] This man was Bob Proctor. Ten years later, I became one of the consultants with Proctor Gallagher Institute.

Honestly, I never saw the obvious connection between different passions that I pursued through life. My initial motivation was to protect and to improve the safety and quality of life for my family and myself. I loved the growth that came with study and the application of the lessons I had learned. I started being somewhat comfortable with uncertainty on the outside because I began to establish balance on the inside. This motivation pushed me both during my days in school and later on in business. However, the connection between different things I was learning was never clearly visible.

Suddenly, something interesting began to happen. The lessons I learned from being bruised in training were somehow manifesting in the books I was reading, and while studying and applying certain principles of "personal development." This did not happen only once, but it became a sort of a weird repetition thing. It was a complete paradoxical correlation between "modern" western philosophies of success and an ancient eastern warrior art. Though completely different on the surface, both were teaching the same principles. They are similar to the concept of yin and yang—describing how seemingly opposite or contrary forces may actually be complementary.

When you grow up with a background like mine you become obsessed with understanding how much "destiny" plays into your life, and how much we are truly the creators of our present. I personally couldn't connect to all the resources that spoke about earning big money fast. If you feel empty and win the lottery, congratulations—you are now an empty rich person. That is why I spent thousands of hours trying to understand and figure out how to live a life filled with joy and purpose; trying to figure out what my role is in creating the difference between surviving and striving, be it in the classroom, the office, the *dojo* (training hall) or on the street.

And when you begin searching for answers, they begin to appear everywhere. I learned about goals, desire, faith, and paradigms. I turned my back on my work as a clinician and returned to university to study something completely different. I got a job that I loved. I achieved some financial success, earning around forty times more than I did before. This was not my goal but rather only a byproduct of who I had become. I could have titled this book: *How I Earned Forty Times More Than I Used To,* and it could have been a way bigger hit. However, the true value was in who I have become in the process.

I began chasing the parallels between what I learned studying western philosophies of success and ancient eastern practices of martial arts while being a manager in the healthcare industry. If I discovered a lesson from one source, I would immediately begin searching for how this lesson might apply, in different form, in the other source.

I began to realize that all these lessons somehow come together to answer one of three basic life questions—questions that must be answered if we are to pursue a life of growth and happiness. I began to share these questions and principles in speeches to students and colleagues. I have also used them for my coaching clients, younger martial arts students, as well as for my employees.

Before this book goes any further, let me come clean about something. I am far from reaching my own inner mastery—my black belt—so to speak. There are thousands of people (at least one hundred that I know personally) who have a better understanding of personal development and the work of Bob Proctor, Earl Nightingale, and Napoleon Hill than I do. Likewise, there are thousands of people that have a much better understanding of Bujinkan, the composition of ancient Japanese martial arts of ninjas and samurais. I am just someone who is lucky enough to have experienced both worlds in parallel over the course of a decade (and still ongoing) and that experience has expanded my own understanding of life from different perspectives.

Whether you have practiced martial arts or studied human development, or you have never done either, you will enjoy this book. You will find the stories and lessons interesting, and most importantly, relatable. While many of these lessons can be found in greater depth and dimension in other books, some of which I mention later, I promised myself to only write about the things I have actually experienced, and in a way that I understand them.

Here's to you finding your answers.

—Ana

Three Questions

You are free to read this book starting from any of the three sections. However, take note that each section is equally important and is connected to the others. Chapters within sections are interconnected and sequential. Like pieces of a puzzle, the parts of this book must be put together so that we may answer the three important questions. But please note: this book is not a theoretical piece. Rather, it is meant to serve as motivation for you, the reader, to go out and play, to test the principles, and to make the best of your journey. When we play, we grow, and playfulness is the essence of life.

Whenever I found myself personally lost or stuck in life, I would always return to the basics. After more than a decade of study and training, regardless of the topic or the audience, I always begin with one of these three essential questions:

- Where am I going?

- Where am I now?

- Who am I, truly?

If you are a student of human and transformational development, you will know that all the greatest authors largely navigate in the world of these three basic questions. Setting goals answers the question of where we are going. Paradigms represent where we are now. And finally, self-image speaks to who we are.

Now let us observe the martial arts aspect. Bujinkan is an organization that represents a composition of Japanese martial art schools of ninjas and samurais that are more than one thousand years old. Dr. Masaaki Hatsumi, our own *Sōke,*[2] introduced the basics of an art form referred to in Japanese as, *Ten Chi Jin Ryaku no Maki.* This roughly translates to *the strategies or principles of heaven, earth, and man.* These three aspects—heaven, earth, and man—are inseparable. Man is shown as being connected to both heaven and earth, with his feet on the ground and his head in the sky. In this representation, man is accountable to both the earth (nature) and the laws of heaven.

In this relationship, Heaven and Earth can both exist without man; however, man cannot exist without the other two. This is why it is vital to understand and form relationships with both. We must practice all three parts so that we may understand the fundamentals of different schools that we start to learn at the later stage. It should be mentioned that all of these basic techniques come from various schools just as all fundamental life strategies come from our various experiences. Here, they are extracted and systematized for the purpose of understanding the basics.

The first section of this book is titled "The Principles of Heaven." Chapters within this section serve to answer the question, *where am I going?* This section will discuss our purpose, vision, and goals. This section also speaks about the need to define our inner

---

[2] Sōke is the grand master of martial arts school.

values and, importantly, how to go about it. One chapter discusses *universal value*. Other chapters describe the importance of having vision, the necessities of proper goal setting (and goal achieving), and why failing is an integral part of the process.

The second section is titled "The Principles of Earth." It seeks to answer the question, *where am I now?* This section describes our limitations, the paradigms we have formed that stop us from progressing to where we would like to be. We will speak about the importance of understanding space, about control, and about the importance of our experiences. The notion of earth describes our relationship with the world around us, and each chapter discusses how to better understand the connections we develop over the course of our lives.

The third and final section is titled "The Principles of Human." In this section, we aim to answer the question, *who am I, truly?* The chapters in this section describe our own mental faculties, the importance of perseverance over persistence, having the right attitude, and the antidote to pain. The strategies of human help us understand and expand our own capabilities to the benefit of our own development, and also for the development of the world around us. Remember, we do not exist as independent units in this world; we are all interconnected to heaven, to earth, and to one another.

Understand? Good. Play!

—Dr. Masaaki Hatsumi,
Bujinkan Sōke

The Principles of Heaven

Chapter I – Values 3

Chapter II – Vision 9

Chapter III – Willingness. 16

Chapter IV – Failure 22

CHAPTER 1

Values

If I were to ask you what your values are, what would you reply? Don't you find it a little bit weird that many well-known organizations across the world state their values publicly yet we, as individuals, are not encouraged to define our own?

Most of my values came from the strong, powerful women who raised me. My grandmother brought up her siblings after her own mother died very young, and she married a man for love despite the fact that this was not only exceedingly rare at the time, but it was also frowned upon. She was a girl from a prosperous family who suddenly found herself living a tough village life. They lived poorly on only what grandpa was able to earn, causing people to gossip and mock her. When women made fun of my grandma for wearing only one headscarf, she would always answer proudly: "I have lots of headscarves, but this one is my favorite!" Proud and strong as she was, she endured and built a family with my grandfather, providing a home and an education to all three of her children. She was a fighter to the end, even with a mastectomy and breast cancer spreading to most of her body. Her legacy lives on to this day through another person who I know even better than my grandmother—my mom.

My mother was born around the end of WWII. She was the first in our family to finish university, she didn't marry until her mid-thirties, and she had a child after the age of forty—she broke a lot of norms in those days. She kept our house together during times of war and great crisis. Since my father was hardworking and often away, including weekends, my mom brought up my brother and I while managing a job, maintaining a home, and keeping everything together.

I learned many things from my parents—how to do laundry, or how to wind coils on electrical transformers, for example. But what they really instilled into my DNA were certain values; saying what you mean and meaning what you say, taking responsibility for your life, and doing the right thing, even when no one is looking.

Values represent our fundamental beliefs. They help us to determine what is important, and at the same time, guide us to act in a certain way. There are universal values that are common for everyone, and there are personal values that make each of us distinct. This section of the book is about goals, purpose, and vision and we can only talk about our greatest aspirations and dreams if we understand what values reside at our core. If you want to set proper goals and strive towards your purpose, you must first define your own values.

Universal values are very important, and there is one that stands out from others because it is not morally relative. Jack Hoban writes about this value in his book *Ethical Warrior*.[3]

---

[3] Jack Hoban is a subject matter expert for the U.S. Marine Corps martial arts program, Bujinkan Dai Shihan (15th Dan in Bujinkan), and a published author.

This universal value is *life*. He refers to it as the Dual-Life Value Theory. Dual-life principle describes the sanctity of all life. All life is equally important, and we must treat all life the same. The lives of our loved ones are as important to us as our own life, if not more. However, we must understand that the lives of other families (even those of our enemies) are as important to them as our family's lives are to us. Grasping this concept opens a door to common understanding and to a place where peace may reside.

My own teacher once told me that first and foremost I study martial arts to protect myself. Then I study to protect others *from* myself. And finally, in the end, I study to protect others from themselves. I believe this is the definition of a true protector and a true warrior.

In 2018, many years after the bombing of Serbia (which I experienced at the age of twelve), I met a man at a Proctor Gallagher Institute consultant training event. We had an amazing discussion of personal growth and he also told me that his work took him to Serbia many years ago. But my heart stopped when he told me that he was a US Air Force pilot. It took me few seconds to connect the dots; the man standing before me was flying one of the planes that bombed my country twenty years before! This man flew the airplanes that caused my bones to shiver every day for months, and that could have easily ended my life and the lives of my family members.

It was an experience I cannot easily describe. We were both somewhat uncomfortable. But as the conversation progressed, we each learned that we were more alike than different. We each had similar desires and aspirations. He told me that the only reason he became a military pilot was because he loved flying but couldn't afford flight training on his own. The military financed his training, and soon after, on beautiful spring nights in 1999, he flew his plane in the skies above me.[4] I understood right there on the spot that wars are a result of people not understanding dual-life value, the sanctity of all life. More often than not, they are brainwashed into believing that by killing innocent civilians, they are somehow protecting other civilians. Or even worse, they are protecting the greatness of a nation. However, I also learned that most people in this world are good in their essence and they all have the same desires—love, purpose, and belonging.

Whether a soldier or civilian, you can still use this universal value in your daily life. There are those who still believe that humans of a different race, different sexual orientation, or different religion deserve to live a less valuable life than others. This is absolute BS! No life is more important than any other life. We are all human beings and we all deserve the right to live a decent and purposeful life.

In addition to universal values we also have personal values that are specific to each of us. Personal values serve as our guiding light, illuminating the way towards our goals and purpose. I came to this realization after experiencing one of several crises in my life. I had just missed a big promotion and I felt completely lost. The usual goal-setting techniques didn't seem to work for me this time.

But then, something clicked. How could I think about my vision and goals if I didn't define my values? The first thing I did was to list the values that caused certain emotions within me— values that I found important. I began grouping them by writing down similar values and choosing one that represented them as a group (for example: *honesty*, *integrity*, and *responsibility*—I

---

[4] I found out later that his plane was not bombing, but was refueling other planes, which gave me a sense of relief.

grouped these under the word *integrity*). For three full days I worked on this list until I had the ten most important values that spoke sincerely to my heart.

Now that I had my list of ten values, I needed to turn them into ten actions. All of these personal values can be morally relative until they are transformed into actions that dictate how you act every day and who benefits from them (Simon Sinek[5] always claims that values are verbs, not nouns).

My value list went like this:

- **JOY**: I feel love and joy in daily things

- **GROWTH**: I learn something new every day, and everyone I meet can be a teacher

- **PRESENT**: I live in the present and look forward to the future

- **PERSEVERANCE**: I work patiently towards my goals knowing that eventually they will come true

- **DECISIVENESS**: I am focused on my tasks and stick to my decisions

- **ADAPTIBILITY**: I welcome and celebrate every experience

- **FAIRNESS**: I am as loyal to others as I am to myself

- **INTEGRITY**: I say what I mean and mean what I say

- **SERVING:** I serve others daily

- **COMMUNITY**: I set apart time every day for the people that are close to my heart

---

[5] Simon Sinek is the international bestselling author of *Start with Why.*

Having grasped the universal value and having defined your own personal values (in accordance with the universal value) you can begin thinking about your own purpose and goals. Your goals must correspond with your values. You cannot make a goal that you don't feel deep in your heart is the right goal for you. Your values can help you when choosing where you want to work, when choosing a partner, or when choosing how you approach certain issues in life. After creating my list, I made an important decision about my career and I have never looked back since.

> Rather than love, than money, than fame,
> give me truth.
>
> —Henry David Thoreau

CHAPTER II

Vision

I started to behave as a person who already had a rank until one day I would arrive there and actually become the rank.

Almost ten years ago I had a vision of going abroad to study. For an eighteen-year-old considering how to begin a career, that might be a normal desire by any standard. But I was an already graduated dentist changing the course of my career just as I was starting it and applying to business school abroad—I had no idea where to begin. And as if things weren't challenging enough, at the time I was working in a private dental practice in a small city in Serbia and sleeping on a mattress on the floor of a colleague.

One could argue whether this was a vision or pure craziness. My parents had no doubts about what they thought it was. (Looking back, I completely understand why.) They told me I had to look at the reality of the situation, and consider shooting for something "more logical." Usually, this kind of a comment would be enough to completely discourage me. But this time, I somehow decided to ignore it completely. Even I was surprised at having not given in to my parents' arguments. I had a goal I wanted to achieve, but I had no idea how to achieve it. I was blind to the fact that I needed almost thirty thousand euros to achieve this goal while my entire family lived on an income of around four hundred euros per month.

You know how they say: *if you want something really hard, it will absolutely come true…* Well, this was not the case. I failed to receive a scholarship, so I was unable to enroll. I was devastated! Knowing that I might not be able to escape this situation really broke me. I made a decision to quit my job. I moved back in with my parents in my hometown, and began working part time as a dentist and part time winding coils on electrical transformers. On a good day, I would take home around twenty euros. Most days it was half of that. My vision of business school and a new career was still in the back of my mind. Everywhere I turned, I would see something that reminded me of the chance I didn't get. It was killing me. After a few months of anger, self-pity, and disappointment, I decided to re-apply.

I can still remember where I was when I got the email informing me that I had received the scholarship. I remember turning off my computer, then turning it back on again to make sure the email was still there (as if it could magically disappear). I could not have been happier! However, only part of my goal was complete as I still needed money to live abroad. At first, my family, once again, thought I should pass on the opportunity. But this time, instinct told me that sometimes in life you get only one shot, and I had a strong feeling that this was mine. After all, I was so close! I told my family that I would find a way, and that I'd made my decision. In the end, they fully supported me. We decided that I should accept the position, and then we all began to think about how to come up with the money.

And then something strange happened. Once I made a decision and accepted the position, things just started to line up. At the time, my father was producing machines for venetian blinds. Up until that point, he had never managed to sell any. Suddenly, he had two buyers within a month! This is how I got enough money to pay for the first two months of my new life. I left home for Italy. Small amounts of money continued to come over the next nine months, until I finally found a paid internship, graduated with my master's degree, and secured a job in Switzerland.

Unconsciously, I had followed strategic rule number one: your vision (and consequent goals) must excite you and scare you at the same time. It should be something that you have no idea how to achieve, yet something that is meaningful to you.

If you have a vision of how you want your life to be in the future it becomes easier to establish proper goals that can bring you closer to it. The purpose of the goal is not to get more; the purpose of the goal is to grow and to draw on something within you that you didn't know was there. And as we grow, we improve our vision and change our goals. That is all part of the beautiful process of life. Goal creation is an artistic process in itself because we invest our very beings for our creation; we give physical and mental effort, and we give the most valuable and scarcest resource of all, our time.

To form a good vision and corresponding goals, you sometimes have to dig deep. When you are young, it is fairly easy to have grand visions and establish scary goals. Ask any youngster what their goals are, and you'll find out—they dream big. But when you grow up, it becomes more difficult to draw that scary vision from within. We become more "realistic" and go for more "logical" results. There is only one cause for why we do this: *paradigms*.

Paradigms represent our own operating systems that run on inner beliefs of who we are, what are we capable of, and how far are we getting every single day. Paradigms are a multitude of habits that have exclusive control over our behavior, for the majority of our behavior is habitual. For the most part, we are not born with our paradigms. They are instilled in us by our parents, teachers, and relatives who themselves also run on their own operating systems (or systems of belief). If we do nothing to replace our paradigms they will stay in place for the rest of our lives. They will govern both our successes and our failures, and they will govern our own logic.

Paradigms are the reason most of us never dare to go for the goals that actually matter to us and eventually end up having the same results over and over again. If you want to change your end results, you must install a new operating system—you must alter your *paradigm*—in order to change what is logical to you. As stated previously, paradigms control your logic! For you, it might be completely illogical to start a new business. But for someone else it can be a completely normal or insignificant task. It all depends on which paradigm we hold. Furthermore, our grown-up versions always think based on our current results and possibilities, which only brings more of the same results in the future. But when we are young, we think based on our inner desires without observing what is actually going on around us; we observe things from a position that we have never been in before, which is completely illogical! But this mentality is exactly what is necessary to form a good goal; the vision must be based on our inner desires. We need something that is coming from the inside out.

Once we create that vision and set a clear goal, there is a certain way we must treat the goals we have established. I studied paradigms for quite a while, but I never understood how much they keep us from progressing. However, on a Sunday some years ago there was a moment where everything came together.

It's funny how these moments often come with seemingly insignificant thoughts or events. I was just given a new rank in my dojo, and I was reminiscing about the bad feelings that came every time I was in this position. You see, usually in martial arts you must accomplish certain tasks in order to achieve a rank. There are certain techniques such as punches and throws that you need to know. After you have successfully learned all the required techniques, there is a ceremony where you demonstrate your knowledge, and then you are awarded a rank. It is like an exam that you pass and are given a grade for. Makes sense, right? Bujinkan is a different story.[6]

In Bujinkan, sometimes you are given a rank during regular training *before* you actually deserve it. Imagine for a moment being in a workplace on a normal Wednesday and out of nowhere you are awarded a promotion that you haven't earned. Everyone is congratulating you but inside you are scared because you have no idea how to do the job in the first place. For me, receiving ranks in Bujinkan felt like this, and I hated it. At times this caused me to pause my training for months, sometimes even a year, because I could not handle the internal pressure. Every time I stepped on *tatami* I felt as if everyone was judging me and I wanted to remove the belt altogether and train without it. I was a beginner with a black belt, and my mind couldn't handle it.

On this particular weekend, I was reading a book on the train on my way to my training (a roughly two-hour commute). I was at peace as I read, until reading the following: "You need to start thinking from the goal, not to it." I read the sentence again. "You need to start thinking *from* the goal and not *to* it." Although I

---

[6] Dai Shihan Duncan Stewart has a great explanation of this concept (Sakizuke). You can find out more about it at the end of this book.

read this sentence at least twenty times before, somehow it was different now. I began to ask myself, what if the thing I dreaded the most was actually working for me without my knowledge?

I began thinking about how I behaved every time I was awarded a new rank. I started to work harder. I was reading more. I started behaving as a person who already *had* a rank (because I did). Then, one day I would arrive and actually *become* the rank. Usually, that would be the moment they would give me a new rank and the process would start all over again. It was a genius idea!

This is strategic rule number two: start looking at your goal as if you have already achieved it. This requires an ability to get there mentally. How do you feel achieving the goal, what is happening around you, and how does it influence your life? Once you have developed this picture successfully, you need to look back and trace the steps you need to take today in order to arrive at your goal tomorrow. Don't make the mistake of waiting for the perfect circumstances to align—start where you are right now.

For all this to happen our goals need to be clearly defined, written on a piece of paper, with a clear deadline. There must be a decision from our side to commit towards achieving these goals; commit with our thoughts, our feelings, and most importantly, with our actions. The razor's edge in the art of achieving goals is constant and continuous daily action. In martial arts, nobody asks, "Are you studying martial arts?" Instead, we ask, "Are you *practicing*?" That is strategic rule number three: a committed decision must be followed by daily action.

This requires an insane amount of willingness and discipline—the kind that wakes you up every morning and sends you back to sleep every night thinking about the goal and knowing that you are on your way there. It took me over five years to achieve my vision of living abroad, working the job I love, and having a secure life. It took me fifteen years to visit Japan for the first time as a practitioner of martial arts. And these were not very clear goals from the beginning. They started years before as tiny pictures in my mind, growing into an unshakeable vision over time. They survived thanks to a great deal of willingness.

> If I want to be free, I have to be me. Not the "me" I think you think I should be, not the "me" I think my parents think I should be, not the "me" I think my kids think I should be. If I want to be free, I have to be me.
>
> **—Bob Proctor / Bill Gove**

CHAPTER III

Willingness

What happened in the time between when I was sleeping on a mattress on the floor and sitting in the VIP section of that seminar room at the Marriott hotel?

It was October 2016, and I had just landed in Frankfurt from a business trip that included Shanghai, Ningbo, and Taipei. It was early on a normal Sunday morning, but I was in a hurry and my heart pounded as I looked for the nearest taxi. I got a ride, and within thirty minutes was in front of the Marriott hotel. About an hour later I was in the VIP section of a seminar room—a room full of people dressed to the nines—eagerly waiting for the seminar to begin. I was excited because, to begin with, at this seminar I was going to meet my personal hero, a man who inspired me to completely change my life. It was also exciting because just a few years before, I could have not even afforded the taxi ride that brought me here. The only thing I had back in those days was a vision scribbled on a piece of a paper and a strong willingness to endure.

My experience taught me that when we set upon the quest to achieve something, we will invest a lot of our time and energy into that quest. This requires that our goal be worthy of the things we willingly give up. This means we must all think twice about what is the vision that will get us up early every single morning to work towards its attainment.

The purpose to which we are surrendering is ultimately what we live for. Some say follow your passion, some say follow your gifts; I believe you need to have a long-term vision and follow your clearly established goals. Only you know what works best for you, but I cannot stress enough how important is to have a clearly defined future that is worthy of hard work each and every day.

In personal development coaching, there are two questions that are crucial to determining how to establish worthy goals. First, *are you able to achieve it?* As people we are able to do incredible things. When we are determined to accomplish something, we find resources and ways to make it happen. You wouldn't even consider that goal if deep in your heart you didn't feel that you might achieve it. But there is a second question that is even more important, and it's very simple—*are you willing?* Are you willing to do whatever is necessary to get closer to your goal and become this new person? Are you willing to endure, to invest yourself and your time, and to persevere? Are you willing to put yourself out there without knowing the result for sure?

My advice: Don't enter the arena if you are not willing to bleed. This book is a collection of different lessons I experienced over the last decade, but it also draws from experiences of my clients, employees, and young martial arts students. The two biggest barriers that prevent people from moving forward are either undefined or mis-defined goals, or an unwillingness or fear to do whatever is necessary to reach them.

In Bujinkan training we would often get people who show up wanting to become ninjas. They want to learn the secrets of being invincible or of how to manipulate others by physical or mental powers. Many people come for the first time asking to learn *kuji kiri* (hand gestures that have certain religious symbolism, but in practice are about increasing our own levels of mental awareness). Kuji kiri is not some magic. It is about accessing a certain mental state, a certain feeling. However, feelings must be attached to our own experiences. That is one of the rare things you cannot simply show up and pay for. As a result, many of these people would not stay in training long. This is the first sign that we are dealing with "instant warriors"—people who want to achieve the *feeling* without going through the *experience*; who want it right here and right now with little or no effort.

Similarly, we have many participants in our personal development courses searching for secrets and expecting significant changes after only a few days. I have met people who watched *The Secret* (a 2006 movie that re-launched the personal development industry) and asked, *why am I not getting what I want?*

The difference between fine wine and wine that tastes bad is not only the grape—it is the process used to make it. Instant warriors want to skip the process. Trust me, if you skip the process you will get the cheap, bad tasting results. Same works for wine maturation and same works for your own "maturation." This process is messy; my own included heavy loneliness, many sleepless nights, sacrificing relationships and, last but not least, losing heart. There is nothing glorious or elegant about the process that one must go through on the way to making their vision a reality. The glory comes in knowing who you have become after surviving and reaffirming to yourself that you made it to the other side stronger and more determined, with a new twinkle in your eyes. But the process itself is dirty and messy; don't ever doubt that.

If you are not willing to do the things other people do not like to do, in order to achieve the things that other people don't achieve, then maybe you don't really want that goal at all. Maybe you just *think* you want it. If it's not worth your blood, sweat, and tears, then don't make it your goal.

> *"Successful people are influenced by desire for pleasing results. Failures are influenced by the desire for pleasing methods and are inclined to be satisfied with such results as can be obtained by doing things they like to do."*[7]

Which one are you?

To achieve what the writer calls "pleasing results," we need impeccable habits. In order to form these habits, we must be willing to exercise certain behaviors repeatedly until they become habitual. This is what we do most often in training or coaching—*we form the right habits.*

We repeat the basic movements over and over. White belt, green belt, black belt—it doesn't matter. We train the basics again and again until we are exhausted. True masters of the skill spend years practicing certain movements in order to ingrain them deeply in their subconscious; the movements become a natural part of the body and mind—they become *habits.* In many other areas of learning, repeating the basics over and over creates a master. The reasoning behind it is very simple.

Repeating new ideas over and over reshapes our patterns of thinking, and as a consequence, our behavior and results are reshaped as well. We are creatures of habit, and when you change your habits, you automatically change the creature. This is not

---

[7] Albert E. N. Gray, *The Common Denominator of Success*

rocket science, but rather, the simple rule of cause and effect. Change the cause, and the effects change themselves.

Becoming a master of anything requires a solid understanding of basics before we can move on to more complex movements or ideas. Every painting, no matter the complexity, consists of many basic brush strokes. The mastery lies within the understanding and application of the basics. Every martial-arts technique consists of only a few basic movements and strikes, but the complexity lies within a combination of basic elements. Every combination requires a deep understanding and repetition of the basics.

The secret is that there are no secrets. If we want to have lasting efforts, we need impeccable habits! In order to persevere in creating these habits, we must have a big goal! If our goals are big enough, we will invest the required effort to accomplish them. But in order to get something, we must first give.

This is why success seems unreachable to many people. Many people today are unwilling to do the same thing over and over with the faith that eventually they will reach their goal and accomplish their vision. This is perseverance. If you want it right here and now without putting in the effort, you don't really want it. Moving towards your goal when the chances of success are unknown, having faith that one day you will get there—this is what a purposeful life is all about.

What happened in the time between when I was sleeping on the mattress on the floor and sitting in the VIP section of that seminar room of the Marriott hotel? Like fine wine, it was a process of maturation. My new daily habits included focusing on my clearly defined goal, waking up every morning for three years and listening to recorded seminars on YouTube, working on my self-image, and eventually investing my first savings on a professional coach. My first coach was YouTube, which proves that willingness is the only thing you need in order to get started. And more importantly, you need to use the power of cumulative effect. Like saving money, a few dollars a week is not much at first. But as the years pass by, you will have accumulated a significant amount. I studied for about an hour every day. It was not much in the beginning, but after three years it was over a thousand hours of learning. Willingness was what made all the difference.

The seminar at the Marriott was the day I first met Bob Proctor. The moment I shook his hand, I set a new goal of becoming one of his consultants. After a few years, that goal came true as well.

If your goal is worthy of you, you will do what it takes. If you are afraid of failing, you are not alone.

> I never ask myself if I am worthy of my dream. I always ask myself: is my dream worthy of me?
>
> **—Mary Morrissey**

Chapter IV

Failure

*Right there, in that moment, when all we could afford
were two light bulbs on a month's salary, my father started
a business in the bedroom.*

We are born with only two fears: the fear of sudden strong noise and the fear of falling. We develop other fears over the course of our lives, but these two are the fears that we have from the very start of our journey. We are literally hardwired for failure before we are even aware of ourselves. When I was a medical student, we would visit the nursery where we could witness the full peculiarity of life as it is from the moment we take our very first breath. Our professor would demonstrate a human reaction to the fear of losing ground by slightly disturbing the bed mattress. As soon as he would do that, the baby would stretch their tiny arms to the sky and grab for the air as much as possible. Of course, our fear of losing ground has a different meaning later in our life. It is not a biological reaction to protect us from death, but it comes very close. Fear is real and will follow us each step of the way.

The moment we decide to go towards something there is a movement in our mind. First, there is a reason to move. Then, there is a decision followed by an action. If our mind delays the movement, no action will follow, and no result will occur in the outside world. In every movement, three different things are engaged: your conscious mind (the thinking mind), your subconscious mind (the emotional mind), and your body (the executor).

The conscious mind (the thinking mind), is a decision-making mind. This part of our mind has the ability to reason, to accept and reject an idea, and to change our course of action. We use the conscious mind when we establish our vision, define goals and when we want to move in a new direction. Think of it as a steering wheel, and how it can influence the direction of your car. Through our conscious mind we develop our six mental faculties: imagination, will, reason, intuition, perception, and memory. These faculties serve us daily.

The subconscious mind (or the emotional mind) is the temple of our behavior. It has no ability to reject or reason with anything, it accepts anything that the conscious mind gives it as an absolute truth, and it forms patterns of our behavior (paradigms). It is tasked with keeping us on course at a certain speed. When mastered properly, the subconscious mind helps us execute daily tasks without too much conscious thought, and it gives us proper habits that make us highly productive and successful. It is a fantastic servant, but a horrible master. So, if our habits are not good and our behavior is poor, the subconscious mind makes us anxious, stressed, and unhappy. Your entire life is made of the relationship between these two parts of your mind.

In the end, we have the body as the executor of the two. You can observe it a bit wider than a physical body and call it action.

Actions determine our results in the outward world. Having a vision is worth nothing if you don't do anything about it. Only when you understand the relationship between the three can you begin to understand why you move, what parts of you are engaged, and what results this structure can cause. Movement requires us to shift to a place of imbalance in order to find new balance.

Imbalance makes us fearful, and that is normal. When the baby starts learning how to walk, it falls multiple times, it bangs its head or hurts other parts of the body. And yet no one has ever seen a baby quit. Every baby learns how to walk, sooner or later. By observing babies, you can learn three very important lessons:

- The moment you begin to move, there is a risk of falling

- Failure will make you creative in finding new ways to move

- Repeated failure re-confirms your determination towards your goal

Because we have it since birth, it is safe to assume that falling (or failure) is an integral part of absolutely any effort we make. If you ever go to judo, aikido, or any martial arts training, the first thing they teach you is how to fall safely. The mats in the dojo are there so that the moment you step on them, you understand two things: first, in this room you will fall; and second, it is required that when you fall you get back up. We learn break falls and rolls in order to absorb the impact and distribute it throughout our body so as to not injure ourselves. But more importantly, we learn these things so we can maintain our movement and keep going.

Falling to achieve our goals or falling short in our endeavors is no different. If you ever failed in anything (and I bet you did) we can agree that it hurts, and it can discourage us from proceeding with our movement.

If you want to move forward in life you have to start being somewhat comfortable with imbalance. Only through imbalance can we eventually find new balance. The problem is that we are not comfortable with imbalance in any area of our lives. We like knowing things for certain, and we are definitely not happy outside of our comfort zone.

The bigger the purpose the easier it becomes to face the fear. If you do want to move, you need a reason big enough to shift you to a place of imbalance. This is the first lesson we learn in coaching—that your vision must be big enough to excite and scare you at the same time so that you will be committed to moving towards it. Only this type of dream can make you consciously accept moving to a place of imbalance or insecurity.

I know what you might be thinking: if you are a bit more realistic and don't strive for big things, failure is less likely to happen. You can play it safe hoping that tiptoeing will get you safely to your deathbed, only to realize that you blew the only chance that was given to you to make the best out of your life. Failure is the price we pay for daring to move, and we are designed to move.

When sanctions happened in former Yugoslavia, everything failed. My parents, both of whom worked in state factories (public entities were common in communist countries), lost their jobs with two small children to feed. They had done everything right, finishing university and getting great state jobs. I know my western friends cannot understand what it's like when the entire system that is designed to protect and provide safety for you crumbles down around you. So right there, in that moment, when all we could afford were two light bulbs on a month's salary, my father started a business in the bedroom. We started producing transformers from scratch: my dad with the help of my mum, my brother, and me.

I was eight years old when we started this business. For me it was like a game. The game was to see who could produce the most transformers in two hours. Then in four. I began to learn something about money and how to earn it. I learned the struggle of staying late until the job is done. I can still remember the smell of tin, glue, and copper. When you have a family business, you don't stay until the clock says it's over, you stay until the job is done and the delivery is on its way. By the time I was sixteen years old, I was the fastest transformer winder in our company. And by that time, we had several other people working with us. I learned that my speed had little to do with skill, but had everything to do with the fact that I was very committed to our family business. Because my family worked for our business to survive.

My parents could have taken us back to the village and never provided us with an education, yet they dared to *move*. I could have stayed in Serbia hoping to find a decent job at some point and accept living forever in my parents' house, yet I dared to *move*. Knowing that I would experience adversity regardless of how big or small I played motivated me to maintain my vision and refuse to shape it to the current reality just so I would avoid failure.

The purpose of failure is to make you more balanced, more creative, and to re-affirm your commitment towards your vision and goals. Do your best to embrace the imbalance and keep moving forward.

Movement starts with a succession of imbalances brought about by one's desire to walk.

—**Dr. Kacem Zoughari**

The Principles of Earth

Chapter V – Space 29

Chapter VI – Paradigms 33

Chapter VII – Control 40

Chapter VIII – Experience 45

Space

This coin has two different sides. On one side of the coin, the surface is rough, and it reads "react." And on the other side, the surface is smooth, and reads "respond." This reminds the owner of the coin to understand where the space is and move in order to give the best response.

In our training we talk a lot about *kukan*. Kukan could be interpreted as *space* or *opening*. This is the space where your opponent is vulnerable. Early in training, you learn a lot about physical space. It is easy to understand how space is an important dimension when it comes to survival. If your head doesn't move out of the way, you get hit. If you do not control your space, someone else takes it. In the dojo we practice and discuss a lot about the distance we create with our movement between the opponent and us by moving our body in the safe position—out of the line of attack. In later training we focus on recognizing the space around us, the opponent, and techniques to control it. Last but not least, we are introduced to techniques that help us create space with our movement and direct our opponent wherever we choose.

Space is an important component in every area of our lives. During the time that I lived in Italy, I shared a one-bedroom apartment with an Italian roommate. There, I learned a lot about space. My roommate was constantly rearranging my things in my part of the room. In the beginning, I would get upset because I thought she was simply messing with my personal belongings. It took me some time to become aware that my overreaction was because she was invading my *space*, and that made me furious. In the animal world it is simple: if you invade the space of another animal, you will get bitten.

When a child becomes a teenager, what is the first thing they ask for? They ask for their own space where parents are not allowed. This is a sign that a child is beginning to establish a new relationship not only with their parents but also with the world around them by establishing their own territory. This space is not necessarily physical. There are also other forms of space. If your manager is constantly micromanaging tasks or your spouse is calling you forty times a day to check your whereabouts—these are also invasions of your space, just in a different form.

Besides understanding that there are many different forms of space (physical, mental, and emotional), there are two other important factors concerning space that we need to learn:

- We need to learn to identify the space between ourselves and others and do our best to control our own space without invading the space of others

- We need to learn to create the space to survive or thrive

What do we teach beginners when they come to train? When the attack comes, the first thing you do is move to a safe space. Only then you respond. Granted, you could react by placing your hands in front of you and closing your eyes. If you have ever actually done that while someone tries to punch you, you know that is not a good idea. It works the same in life. Person that is reacting has no control over their reaction and consequently over the end result; furthermore, this reaction is usually based on our paradigm. Person that is responding has limitless options of the direction they can take. When my clients have finished their coaching sessions, I gift them a coin that was made by the Proctor Gallagher Institute. This coin has two different sides. On one side of the coin, the surface is rough, and it reads "react." And on the other side, the surface is smooth, and reads "respond." This reminds the owner of the coin to understand where the space is and move in order to give the best response.

The third factor is the ability to create space for things that are important to us. We all know that nature abhors a vacuum. When you create space, something automatically fills it. It's the same in the physical world as it is in the spiritual world. The mother of my friend understood that at a very unconscious level. If she wanted a new sofa in her house, for example, she would throw out the old one first. If I asked her why she would throw out the old one before having a replacement she would reply, "If I keep it, it will just stay there forever." Emptying a space creates an urge to fill it.

If you want something or someone in your life you must first create a space for that thing. In chapter seven of this book I mention that I was in love for years, waiting for a particular person. During that time, the space in my head that was designed for my partner was already filled with my crush. During these years, nobody else came along because my mind was already filled.

The moment I let it go, someone new appeared. And it happened within weeks! But I had to clear the space first so that someone new could come in. Always remember, emptiness tests the level of our faith. It is scary and highly uncomfortable to think that we will have empty space for long periods of time, which is why we dread it so much. But it will not long remain empty because the moment you create space you send a clear signal that you expect something to move in to fill it.

This is the first lesson in The Principles of Earth: learn to identify your own space. Then, learn how to control it while not endangering others in the process. And finally, learn to create the space for the vision you want in your life. This will not be easy, because our old paradigm will fight that change with a great force.

> Between stimulus and response there is a space. In that space is our power to choose our response. In our response lies our growth and our freedom.
>
> —Viktor Frankl

CHAPTER VI

Paradigms

But suddenly, in front of all those people, the fearless seventy-year-old leader with fifty years of experience in business began to cry.

When thinking about paradigms, I can't help but to remember a boy named Stefan. His mother first brought him to training twelve years ago. It was not uncommon for parents to bring their children to training because they needed an activity outside of the house, but this situation was different. His mother mentioned that Stefan spent over twelve hours per day playing video games. I can still see him in my mind—a tall, skinny, fifteen-year-old boy with fairly poor social competences. At first, I thought he might have a psychological issue. He would often interrupt sensei, he had a difficult time handling silence, and he would make inappropriate comments in many different situations.

But what's more, when he tried to punch, his body moved in a completely unnatural way. It was obvious that spending so much time on a computer every day had shaped him into a sort of robot (for lack of a better word). With regular training and a lot of effort, we had to completely reshape his habits, his artificial movement patterns, and just as importantly, his social skills.

Stefan was an extreme case, but we do this with everyone who comes to train. It's as if we must clean the bad programs, those that prevent us from growing, out of our operating systems. With regular training we must bring back the three-year-old version of us: natural free movement, natural thinking, and a good and honest heart.

In chapter two I mentioned paradigms for the first time. I stated that paradigms have control over our logic and that in order to change our logic we must change our paradigms. Paradigms represent the mental programs that we receive both genetically and environmentally when growing up. Once old enough we have a set of beliefs and behaviors, and consequently a set of results, all of which ultimately determine our place in the world. Almost everything in our life is connected to some sort of belief that we hold. The only way to change a certain belief is to thoroughly replace it with a new belief. If we want to do this intentionally, this requires us to repeat actions that can change our habits until the new habit patterns are formed and the old ones are completely gone.

Most important of all, paradigms are powerful beyond measure. Whenever you try to change anything about yourself, hell will break lose inside you to prevent this change. So how do we still do it?

Six years ago I got a great job in a dental company, first as an intern, later as an employee, and eventually as a manager. It was my first year, and it was not easy adapting to the new environment. The paradigms I was carrying with me did not help much either. I was six months in when I realized that I did not have good chemistry with the CEO. You know that feeling when you sense something is off, but you don't know what it is? This is exactly what was happening to me.

One day, I got up the courage to go and speak to him. To make a long story short, he told me that he believed I was not a good fit for the company and that he did not think I should work there anymore. I was good at my job, but we didn't match in terms of personality. That was bad news because, while I could fix my performance, changing my personality was a tough one. He did not fire me. I was working with his daughters and we had a good working relationship. But I knew what his statement meant; he was expecting me to quit. Which, under normal circumstances would have happened. But my life at the time was anything but normal.

You see, having a Serbian passport and managing to land a working visa in Switzerland was very difficult due to many legal constraints, and I barely made it. Losing my job would probably mean returning to the country I tried so hard to leave.

After this talk with the owner, I went home crying; I felt devastated. At the time, I was going through the Bob Proctor coaching program, *Thinking Into Results*; this is the same program I am coaching now. I had an amazing coach, Jen Barna, from Sacramento, whom I immediately called. I was about to lose my job and my future altogether. I started crying again.

The following conversation between Jen and myself would be considered crazy by any normal person who does not understand the principles she used. At the time, there was also a big part of me that believed what she was saying was just ... insane. I called Jen, crying, and told her about my day. She remained completely composed. Her face was serious but somehow not worried. She looked at me and said:

"So, the owner of the company does not think you should be working there because you don't match?"

> Me: Yes, I cannot believe this is happening. I worked so hard for this!

> Jen: Let me ask you something. Do you like working for that company at all? Do you like your job?

> After short pause, I responded: Well, yes. I like my job and I think we have a good purpose. And I like living here.

> Jen: Ok, good. Now this is what you are going to do. Write about the current situation on a piece of paper in as much detail as you can. Write about how your boss doesn't like you and how he thinks you need to leave. Write any details about how you dread going to work. Then, take another piece of paper and write the opposite; write how your boss likes your work and appreciates you as a person, and about how you enjoy working there and living where you currently live. Next, take the first piece of paper and burn it. After you have done this, start reading the other paper daily and focus on your mission at work. Think about this picture every single day. Do not skip a day. And Ana, one more thing…

> Me: What?

> Jen: Every time you see your boss, think about one thing you like about him. But it *must* be honest.

After that talk, I was seriously thinking Jen was on drugs and that I had officially reached a new level of desperation for going along with this. But I still decided I was going to try. I was already on the verge of losing my job anyways, so I did what she asked me. I wrote the two notes, one describing the current situation and then the one describing the ideal situation. I burned the first paper in the sink. I started going to work thinking about my mission. Every time I saw the boss, I would think about how dedicated he was to the company and the vision. After the first month, there was no change. But I didn't stop, I continued with this routine daily.

After a while, something interesting began to happen. Somehow, I started to feel more positive about going to work. When I encountered the owner, I would smile when I greeted him. He responded with a smile, too. Things were getting better and I no longer felt like crap as I came to the office each day. I was beginning to understand Jen's genius, but there was no a-ha moment just yet.

A year passed in this effort, and I was still working on the task that was given to me. One day, our company had a big meeting and I was supposed to give an important speech in front of our sales partners from all around the world. I prepared and came to the stage ready to share what my department did for the company and why it was important. I was on fire! I talked about my mission and about the mission of the company. Perfect words were flowing flawlessly out of my mouth. The owner of the company had a smile on his face. He would say something out loud like, "Wow, she *is* good," and continued smiling while I was still lecturing.

When I finished, people applauded for a bit longer than usual. Then, the owner came to the stage. I was happy but I was not prepared for what would happen next. He shook my hand and seemed like he wanted to say something to the audience. But suddenly, in front of all those people, the fearless seventy-year-old leader with fifty years of experience in business began to cry. I will not go into detail about what he said to me afterwards because I believe that some things should be private, but I finally knew that I stumbled upon something amazing. What I discovered was: with proper guidance we can shape our own programing and by doing so, we will shape our own destiny.

I finally understood what happened. Jen was changing my paradigms by simultaneously changing my habits and thought patterns. In turn, this changed my behavior. Once my behavior began to change, my results were not only changing—they were skyrocketing! I finally understood the phrase, "Nothing will change unless you change. Once you change, everything else will!"

This is the true power of paradigms. They control our thinking, our feelings, our behaviors, and our results. That might seem like a bad deal for most of the time, but we can use this power to our own benefit. Today, I have great relationship with the owner of the company. He recently gave me a painting, and on the back was his signature and the inscription, "Für meinen serbischen 'Tank' in Anerkennung der grossen Verdienste." (For my Serbian Tank, in recognition of great merit.) What he considered a personality flaw early on (my direct and strict approach) he now respects and celebrates.

In order to change your paradigm you need to replace it with a new one. You have to change both your thought patterns and your corresponding habits simultaneously. Changing your thought patterns without changing your non-productive habits won't accomplish much. Likewise, trying to change your habits without changing your thoughts creates a yo-yo effect. It is important to follow the process: write out a new paradigm and start behaving as if it is already real. At the same time, begin introducing a new corresponding habit. This might seem simple, but it is far from easy. It requires serious self-discipline, which we will speak about in the next chapter.

Remember Stefan? Within a year of regular training, he flourished. His posture, movements, and his behavior changed completely. He reduced his video game time dramatically and he improved his relationship with his family and friends. He was finally free.

> Paradigms are mental programs that have almost exclusive control over our habitual behavior, and almost all our behavior is habitual.
>
> **—Bob Proctor**

CHAPTER VII

Control

Seconds after I grabbed him, he punched me right in the stomach with his free hand. It wasn't hard enough to seriously injure me but strong enough that I felt it, dropped my hold, and slightly bent over.

In the early days, having a sensei come from abroad to teach was a big deal for us all. We could not afford to visit the seminars in Belgrade or in other countries. Around 2007, we had people coming to practice with us from Greece. Among the first to come to south Serbia was Dai Shihan Adonis Mitrou, and later, his brother Harry. They came to show us how to work more effectively and to demonstrate certain techniques that we could not have seen otherwise. None of us ever had enough money to visit Japan to learn directly from the source of the knowledge.

We were outside practicing some techniques with our partners when a sensei approached me and told me to grab him, offering his arm. I instantly grabbed his arm with both hands (to this day, I have absolutely no idea why I did that). Immediately after I grabbed him, he punched me right in the stomach with his free hand. It wasn't hard enough to seriously injure me but strong enough that I felt it, dropped my hold, and slightly bent over. My partner looked at him a bit shocked and sensei said, "What? She's a black belt. She can take it."

He turned to leave but then stopped, turned back to me, and whispered in my ear, "Don't ever grab with everything you have. And more important, if you decide to do that you have to be ready to let go." Then he left.

There are two things that could be said with almost certainty on the topic of control: we love to have control, and we do not enjoy being controlled. We connect the feeling of control with certainty, and, oh boy, do we enjoy certainty. Of course, there are extremes. There are people who refuse to control anything and there are people who want to assert control over everything.

The lesson he was teaching me was reinforced many times in my life. When we pursue something that really matters to us, we tend to hold on with great force to either the thing we want or to the way to achieve it.

In my twenties, I was crazy in love (like everyone at that age) and it took me four years to let it go. I went through four years of the agony of being hopelessly in love with someone who did not love me back (at that time I refused to see it). I was holding on firmly believing that this was it. The thing is, what I needed was to be loved. What I *believed* I wanted was that particular someone. The solution is never to chase a particular person; you can just go ahead and trust me on this. If you are in your twenties and reading this chapter, this might save you some years of your life. Well, maybe not—you need the experience after all!

As it usually happens, an outside occurrence made me let go. After finally believing that we were settling in as a couple, I was cheated on. For me it was a final deal breaker. Just a few weeks after letting go, someone more suitable appeared in my life. This person loved me for who I was and was someone whom I actually enjoyed being with. My whole emotional life changed, and it took only a few weeks! But I needed to stop grabbing with both hands.

If we hold on to certain people, situations, or ways, we will not be able to control the world around us. Even worse, we will become dependent on the very thing we are trying to control. When people fixate on one road, they lose the sight of the options that exist everywhere else, and with it they lose the freedom to choose along the way.

I cannot remember who said this, but the picture of the control principle is represented perfectly in this idea: if you have the faith to hold your desire on the wide-open palm of your hand, then you understand that only what is truly yours will be found there at any point of time.

If you try to micromanage every step of the way while firmly fixating on a certain method, this is not going to reflect well on your results. And you might get punched in the stomach! This doesn't mean giving up your big vision and your clearly formed goal, it just means do not fixate on the way or the people in order to achieve it. The way will appear, and believe me, it will be the right one. You have to stop being stubborn and just accept it. This never means going the way that speaks against your own values or hurting others. It means stop fixating on having an immediate answer to the question of *how*. The how will appear, but you have to be patient.

Instead, there are things you can and should control. You should control yourself and your focus. By that I mean your thoughts, feelings, and actions should be in line with the goal you set. I don't know any better way to do this than to practice self-discipline.

When Brian Tracy[8] attended a conference, he met Kop Kopmeyer—a legend in the field of success and achievement who had written four books of two hundred and fifty success principles each. Brian asked the author, out of the one thousand principles that he wrote about, which was the most important in order to succeed in life? Kop Kopmeyer responded, "The most important success principle of all was stated by Elbert Hubbard, one of the most prolific writers in American history, at the beginning of the twentieth century. He said, 'Self-discipline is the ability to do what you should do, when you should do it, whether you feel like it or not.'"

When I think about my coaching clients, their success does not depend on the level of service I provide because I serve each of them with the same dedication. Their success depends only on their committed decision towards their goal, their self-discipline, and their willingness to follow through with the program as much as needed in order to get there. If I think about my martial arts training, I see it very clearly. It takes some self-discipline for our students to show up to the dojo on Sunday morning or during the week after eight to ten hours of work. I firmly believe that martial arts represent a great way to master your body and mind and learn self-discipline.

Self-discipline basically means being willing to sacrifice short-term pleasures in order to receive something of higher value. However, the meaning of this particular word is not the same everywhere in the world. In my native Serbian language (with Slavic roots) we use the same word for *sacrifice* that we do for *victim* (*žrtva*). In our culture, sacrifice often means giving up something

---

[8] The book *No Excuses* from Brian Tracy is a really good read if you want to learn more on self-discipline. He has written over seventy books.

to the point of becoming a victim and hence we usually attach a very negative connotation to the word. But in reality, this is not the case. True self-discipline means understanding the difference between what you want *now* and what you want *the most*. When you chase a certain goal, sometimes you must sacrifice an evening of Netflix or a beer with friends. If a goal is very meaningful to you it will not be perceived as *victimization*, but rather, as an investment.

Forget controlling others. Forget controlling the circumstances and methods. Stop grabbing everything with both hands because you are afraid that you might lose it. What slips out of your hands was never yours to begin with. Or, it was yours for the part of your life where it made sense but with your growth it no longer fit, and it was time for you to move on. Focus on yourself, nurture your mind with productive thoughts, and master self-discipline.

What sensei taught me about control had several layers of knowledge that I was able to dissect through years of experience. It influenced my relationships, my work, and my training. It all came with time and with the experience I gained.

Freedom is the only worthy goal in life. It is won by disregarding things that lie beyond our control.

—**Epictetus, Greek Stoic philosopher**

CHAPTER VIII

Experience

"Shut up and train."

Those four words I used to hear on a regular basis growing up. They have shaped me more than many *how to* manuals ever could. In our old dojo it was strictly forbidden to chat in the middle of the training, or for students to interrupt other students in order to "explain" how to execute a technique. There were only two people in the dojo who were allowed to teach others. What do you think was required from the rest of us? You guessed it right: shut up and train. This concept wasn't about us being single-minded or obedient. It was about focusing to get our actual own experience because at the end of the day it does not matter how much you read about ninjutsu, it is only important how much you actually practice (you can replace the word ninjutsu with any other skill).

Why would we come to training with a *talking-too-much* attitude in the first place? Our own school curriculum is designed in a way that it rewards repeating the given information. Remember every test you ever had in school? We grow up believing that repeating what we read means that we understand it. But the very word *education* doesn't mean repetition; *educere,* a Latin expression actually means "to draw out something (from within)."

Our way of education mistakenly leads us to think that reading and remembering the book would lead to understanding of how life works. Succeeded once in a relationship by just reading a book? Became a master in marketing strategy because you have the book with the same name on the bookshelf in your home? Or even better, why do you think dental students line up all their relatives or friends that they can think of once they start practicing dentistry? There are a plethora of books or YouTube manuals on how to drill, so why do you need your mom in the dental chair? Becoming a good dentist requires years of actual experience with real patients, that's why.

In order for something to become part of our subconscious mind and become a true understanding, it has to entail a feeling component and that only comes through experience. Whether you need to call upon your previous experiences or create new ones, experience is what matters at the end of the day. Every experience is there to make you grow and develop understanding. There are two common reasons people usually avoid this process: gaining experience takes time, and the experience itself is not always positive.

The people that don't want to spend time gaining experience are defined as "instant warriors" in my dictionary. Using this expression, I specifically refer to people who want to have the understanding without the process, the talkers who don't like to sweat. It is interesting to see how today we are severely impatient for getting results right here and right now and it seems that many people are not willing to pay the price. Have you ever wondered why Japanese samurai swords are so damn expensive? It's because of the complicated manufacturing process where one repeatedly heats, hammers, and folds the metal over and over again to create a perfect cutting blade. This extensive process of forging and forming the blade is what makes it valuable.

Besides not being willing to invest time, we are also unwilling to encounter negative experiences. This is highly connected to failure, which we discussed in the last chapter in the previous section. There, we learned that failure is integral part of every success. Now, you will be able to understand a bit more why. There is one purpose of negative experiences and it is well described by the concept of trial and error.

The concept of trial and error is well known in cybernetics. Cybernetics, the study of goal-directed systems, explains how goals are specifically reached by having these trial and error moments. There are usually two mechanisms applied here.[9] The first mechanism is where the position of the goal we are reaching for is already known. For example, a missile flies on a winding path already having in its system the location of the target it is trying to reach. As it flies, it feeds information to the central system so that when it is off course the central system can bring it back on the correct path until it reaches the target.

There is also a second mechanism. When we search for a specific target, assuming it exists, we are trying to detect it through a series of different tries until it is located. That means that we are employing the series of missed shots until the target is safely secured. Once the target is reached, only the successful path will be remembered for the next time.

Imagine if a missile was never fired in the first place (or a plane never took off) because it will have some zigzags on its

---

[9] This concept is perfectly described in Maxwell Maltz book, *Psycho-Cybernetics*

path! These twists and turns are necessary and essential in order to reach the target! We are probably the only beings on the planet who record all of our negative experiences and bring them to our consciousness every time we want to have another shot at something. This effectively prevents us from trying again to reach our goals. Negative experience must be perceived for what it represents: feedback that helps us reach the target more effectively next time, and that is all. The moment you actually reach the target, the feedback that has fulfilled its purpose should simply be—forgotten.

Gaining experience is not an easy process, yet it is essential because of the *feeling* aspect it brings with it. You cannot understand love from reading a book—you have to experience it. The feelings of failure and success all come from experience. Feeling is what connects people, as well as what connects our conscious and subconscious minds. That part is openly visible in training.

In martial arts you first learn the basic movements. As time goes by, you begin learning about the feeling that is related to the technique. Often, a technique will be executed on a person and the master will ask, "What was your feeling?" The student will then explain how they experienced the technique. There are two reasons for this. First, because the master wants to see if the student understands the technique. Second, sometimes there is not enough time for a teacher to give the experience to everyone so the explanation is meant for the rest of us to try to grasp how we should execute and feel that technique. This oral transmitting is not perfect. Remember, you cannot gain experience like this, but it helps us understand which feeling we need to have. Then, we try to relive that experience through executing the technique.

Experience is inseparable from feeling; they are two sides of the same coin. We need experience to gain a feeling, and feelings are influencing our new experiences and how we perceive them. Feeling is vitally important as it will imprint anything from our conscious to our subconscious mind.[10] Whether you believe your future will be good or bad, you are putting a strong feeling behind something that still doesn't exist. And once the subconsciousness is imprinted, it automates our behavior towards that image. Our mind is like the earth. The earth doesn't care what we put in it; it will always give us the product of the seeds that we plant.

"Shut up and train" means being focused on your vision, and working towards it by gaining your own experience. Through gaining experience we will begin to develop a new corresponding feeling. That way, we can change our deep systems of belief and consequently change our results.

> You can only understand if you've had the technique done to you. It's like food. You can't describe the taste, but if you've tasted it, you know what it is. You have to personally experience it to understand.
>
> —Dr. Masaaki Hatsumi

---

[10] Neville Goddard talks about this concept in his book *Feeling Is The Secret*

The Principles of Human

Chapter IX – Perseverance 53

Chapter X – Weapons 58

Chapter XI – Attitude 66

Chapter XII – Vital Points 71

Perseverance

The most valuable part of this beautiful present was the tiny inscription written on the back of the framed poem. It read, "The Secret of Ninpo is an honest and strong heart and hard training. Keep going."

My older brother and I started training martial arts around the same time. He trained boxing and judo and would often join us for training in the beginning, but later, not so often. He really liked the training and tried to come back several times, but in the end, as many people do, he stopped coming. After my return from Japan last year, I was excitedly sharing my experience with him and I could feel he was very proud of me. He said to me, "You know, if I could choose only one thing that I admire about you it would be your perseverance. You lasted all these years training and moved to different countries facing many challenges on the road, and yet you never quit. That is impressive." I smiled and replied, "Well, that is *ninjutsu*, isn't it?"

Our martial arts used to be called *Bujinkan Ninpo Taijutsu*, but over time it has changed to *Bujinkan Budo Taijutsu*. When

I speak to people, I just tell them I practice *ninjutsu* because it's easier for everyone to connect it with ninjas and every conversation would usually end there. I know this is not exactly accurate but sometimes there is just not enough time (or will) to explain: "It is the composition of nine schools, some of which are samurai schools and some of which are ninjutsu schools, and no, I am not real ninja, and no, ninjas were not just spy assassins."

But what does this terminology actually mean? The term *ninpo* is made of two characters, *nin* and *ho*. *Nin* can be understood to mean perseverance, stealth, and patience. The character itself is composed of two individual characters that represent a blade placed over the heart. What is the meaning behind it? One meaning is that the blade forces the heart to remain stealthy in order to persevere. Another meaning is that the heart should be as sharp and pure as the sword. The heart under the blade takes on an additional meaning for me—one of being vulnerable and courageous.[11]

With these definitions a ninja would be a person who perseveres—a person who continues on a course of action with courage and vulnerability even in the face of difficulty or with little or no indication of success. It is a person who shows up, goes all in, and continues moving forward.

The second character, *ho*, is translated as *law* in Japanese. In this composition, it takes on the Buddhist meaning and is a bit more complicated. The result of combining it with the first character, *nin,* produces the term *ninpo*. This could be understood as the ultimate and eternal reality of perseverance and stealth, or the philosophy of perseverance. *Ninpo* should not be interpreted in only one way; try to understand its depth in its various meanings.

---

[11] Brené Brown states in her extensive research that the only way to feel joy, love, and belonging is to be vulnerable; we cannot have one without the other.

The true secret lies within the character *nin,* or perseverance. There is a big difference between persistence and perseverance, and this difference can be the deciding factor in the results that we get in life. Persistence is very much celebrated in the western world as a virtue that every successful person needs to have. However, persistence is often times more closely related to stubbornness. A person keeps trying to the point where persistence becomes a goal of its own. A perseverant person, on the other hand, focuses on the end result even if it takes years to accomplish, even when the chances are slim, bordering on non-existent.

What's more, perseverance implies the presence of two other virtues, patience and faith, which are closely connected. Patience demonstrates that we know deep in our heart that what we seek shall be attained, and that means *faith* is present within. This faith is not a blind faith that disappears with the first obstacle; rather, it is a faith that is based on deep understanding. Only a person with strong faith and the right expectations will be patient, knowing that in the end they will achieve their vision. Show me a perseverant person and I will show you a true winner.

If you believe that you are not a perseverant person, please note that no one is born perseverant. You can develop everything you truly want to develop about yourself with time and with the right actions. This is not easy because we have deep underlying beliefs about ourselves that prevent us from growing, and those are the beliefs we must replace. In the same way that you have formed your belief system about the world around you, there is a belief system that you have formed about yourself and your capabilities. We call this belief system *self-image.*[12]

---

[12] Self-image was coined by Dr Maxwell Maltz in his great book *Psycho-Cybernetics.*

What exactly is self-image and how does it work? There are three things you need to know about your self-image. First, no one is born with an image of self. When we are babies, we are not even able to distinguish our parents as separate entities let alone understand ourselves. Little by little as we grow, we begin to be aware and we experience triumphs and failures. We grow up with our parents, relatives, and teachers telling us "truths" about who we are and what we can do. And during this time, no border exists between our consciousness and subconsciousness. As a result, we naturally absorb everything we are taught. With time, we mentally construct a picture of self. Once we reach a certain age, the border between our consciousness and subconsciousness closes in. We are left with an ingrained image that represents an absolute truth about us and we never ever doubt its validity. As the years go by, we start acting as the person we believe we are, regardless of our actual capabilities and potential.

The second important thing to know about self-image is this: we cannot step outside of our self-image regardless of how hard we try or what sort of willpower we invest. If your self-image is that you are a C-grade student and somehow you get an A on a test, the next two grades will be so bad that your grade at the end of the year will still be a C. We have to stay true to our self-image no matter what. It's like a thermostat that does whatever is necessary to keep the temperature in a room set to a certain level at all times. When it's cold, the heat will increase; when it's too hot, the heat will turn off. The temperature will always remain the same.

The third and most important thing about self-image is that we have the ability to change it. In the same way we change our paradigms, the belief system we have formed about the world around us, we can also change our self-image, part of the belief system we have formed about ourselves. We need a new idea of ourselves implemented through according feeling, according behavior, and constant repetition. Our self-image should be in line with the vision we have for ourselves, which is how we should develop it.

To conclude, you can and should become a perseverant person—but this is not enough. In order to live a good life you should also develop an honest and compassionate heart and be able to move towards your goal while being an empathetic human being. My first sensei once gifted me a beautiful framed ninjutsu poem (you can read it at the end of the book). The most valuable part of this lovely present was the tiny inscription written on the back. "The Secret of Ninpo is an honest and strong heart and hard training. Keep going." Keep this in mind while building your self-image.

Developing yourself takes time. Your vision should be designed in a way that you are in it for the long haul. It took me fifteen years to learn what others learn in five. Not because I am slow but because I was in and out of training, had no money for seminars, or because I was moving throughout different cities and countries. Sometimes, I felt like I should quit. But I never did. I believe that you should think twice before you commit to something in life, but once you do, please don't let go. Visiting Japan fifteen years after first starting my training was a dream come true for me. Passing the *sakki* test was an even bigger dream. It might take me another fifteen years to get to the next level, but I simply don't care. The vision I hold is worth it. This is perseverance. This is *ninjutsu*.

> We must have perseverance and above all confidence in ourselves. We must believe that we are gifted for something and that this thing must be attained.
>
> —Marie Curie, Nobel Prize Winner

CHAPTER X

Weapons

I sat with my back turned to the guy with the wooden sword, closed my eyes and thought about my family back home. The next thing I remember was being on the other side of the room, sōke yelling out, "OKEY!" and everyone around clapping. My intuition saved me.

In the dojo, we regularly practice with weapons: knives, wooden swords, short sticks, long sticks, you name it. We observe weapons as extensions of our body and not as separate entities, and there is a good reason for this. The weapon in your hands is only as good as your ability to use it. We learn to use many different weapons and once a person manages the basic postures and movements, they can slowly begin implementing them into their techniques. It is important to learn the basics and practice with weapons, even though some of those weapons are not used today. Why is that? Because we need to understand the essence of the time when these techniques were recorded and passed down to the next generation.

With weapons you learn distance. You learn to spot what's lacking in your technique or balance because weapons reveal the weaknesses in your body movements (*taijutsu*). You learn that you are the master, not the weapon. You also learn to adapt the weapon to your movements and not the other way around (assuming your movements are correct).

As humans we have access to the mental weapons that were given to us very early in life. Here, I talk about tools of the mind rather than tools of the brain. Tools of the brain are the five senses that everyone is familiar with, but tools of the mind are not widely known. These mental tools (or faculties) are perfect, yet they are only as good as our ability to use them. With these mental weapons we can also spot what lacks in our thinking and our reasoning, or deficiency in our focus and will. With time, we learn how to practice and how to adapt them to our own purpose.

Humans have six mental faculties: memory, will, imagination, perception, intuition, and reason. At this point, your vision might require developing one faculty over the other. Choose one, and when you feel that you have mastered it, move on and develop another. You will be the equivalent of a warrior who can win any battle.

Memory – People don't have good or bad memory, rather, we have strong and weak memory. There are hundreds of resources to help you develop a stronger memory. Memory is a muscle, just like your bicep. With daily training it grows and becomes strong. If you do not train it, you will lose it. We develop memory through association. If you want good books on developing your memory you can search for some like Buzan's *The Mind Map Book* or Cooke's *Remember Remember,* among many others.

Will – Will is one of the least understood mental faculties. We often mistake will for willpower. Willpower is a conscious effort to control yourself and your impulses. People normally use willpower to stop or control a bad habit. As such, willpower only gets us so far—because controlling the negative requires so much effort until we are exhausted. Fighting negative habits with sheer force gets you nowhere. *Will* is different. Will gives us the ability to focus on what we want as long as we want it to the exclusion of all outside distractions. It takes practice and it is definitely not an easy task but will represents our focus towards our wants. Our motivation to focus on our vision is bigger and more natural as it requires no force. Your desire should flow naturally to you when you give it space.

If you want to practice will, set aside part of the day where you can sit quietly and think about your goal. Whenever your thoughts move away, gently redirect them back towards your goal. Do not stop or counter your thoughts. They are like a river; stopping them will cause them to flow in other directions. Redirect the flow towards your *want*. This is how you practice focus and develop will.

Imagination – Imagination is responsible for the greatest human achievements of all time—planes, cars, the internet—you name it. Using our imagination properly brings us forward in life, in our thinking, our feeling, and our actions. It has been proven that when a runner simulates a run in their head the same neurological areas of their brain light up as if they were running in real life. That means that your brain considers as real anything you thoroughly imagine, so long as there are feelings attached to the image you hold. Your brain cannot distinguish between you *thinking* of a certain activity in detail and you actually doing it.

How many times have you thought about eating a lemon and suddenly your mouth filled with water?

When I was applying for business school, one of the first things I saw online was a video of the previous generation's graduation ceremony. I would watch this video several times and then go out for a walk. I was imagining myself graduating in that class and throwing my cap in the air. With time, this visualization became so powerful that I would bring myself to tears just by seeing that image in my mind. Three years later, I was actually standing in the same room from the video with my graduation cap in my hands. This time, I felt no excitement. I had lived this moment so many times in my imagination that my mind accepted it as a reality long before it actually became a reality. But the feeling of accomplishment was still there, and it was amazing.

Our imagination is the source of both our greatest power and our greatest challenge because it represents the door to our subconscious mind. This door has a direct impact on our thoughts, feelings, actions, and results. When you visualize something with a strong feeling that supports the image, this is when your emotional mind starts to receive the impulse and reacts accordingly with appropriate behaviors and results. You worry about a certain situation, you project your imagination towards a negative outcome, and it causes anxiety on every level: your thinking, feeling, and behavior. If you visualize getting the job that you wanted, you will start thinking about different ways in which that desire could actually come true. You will start feeling relaxed and enthusiastic and you will actually begin to behave as if you are on your way to getting it. Remember, this is an oversimplified explanation, but it helps us to have a better understanding of how the imagination works.

Reason – Reason represents our ability to think and is therefore part of our conscious mind (the thinking mind). You can take any idea and reason with it to determine whether you want to accept it or reject it. Once you accept the idea, it goes directly to the subconscious mind and becomes a part of your belief system—your paradigm. From that point on, any information you receive about the same topic has to be in accordance with the belief system you hold. Be very aware of what thoughts you choose to accept or reject. They might guide your destiny.

If you look at your current results you can reason that this is how far your capabilities can take you. This produces a feeling that is in line with your current results. This feeling will then produce identical behavior which, in the end, produces more of the same results. Your current results are the product of your previous thinking. If you start thinking based on where you want to be regardless of your current results your thoughts will change, your feelings will change, your behavior will change, and consequently your results will dramatically transform. You cannot improve your results by observing the current reality. This is why reasoning is an important mental faculty.

Perception – Our perception plays a crucial role in our daily life. Every coin has two sides and our ability to see both is very important. The crucial thing to understand about perception is not to ignore one side of the coin! The biggest mistake of all the *be positive* philosophies is that they sometimes teach people to fake it and ignore the negative. Practicing perception means first acknowledging the obvious negatives and then trying to understand where the positives lie. This requires some practice, but it is vitally important. Whatever we are focused on, we will grow more of that thing.

Like a coin, every situation has two sides. Every crisis gives birth to both failures and opportunities. Our task is to acknowledge the obvious crisis and try to identify where the opportunity is. Perception and reason are perfect tools for helping us reach our vision.

Intuition – The original meaning of the word intuition is *to guard* or *to protect*. Gavin de Becker[13] describes intuition as a sort of memory stored in our subconsciousness during our life that communicates to us when we are in danger. He states that our subconsciousness picks up on things that our conscious mind does not register and provides us with insight in dangerous situations.

In Bujinkan we have something called *sakki*—a test that we must go through in order to attain the right to enter more intermediate levels of study, and to eventually start teaching independently. The test looks like this: First, you sit on the ground, close your eyes, and enter a place of calmness. Behind you, a person will stand with a wooden sword, also with their eyes closed. At some point, the person with the wooden sword will send out their intention of seriously hurting you and then attempt to inflict the hit. The person sitting with their eyes closed needs to sense the attacker's intention and move out of the way before being struck.

This test represents the connection between the person giving it and the person receiving it. It shows whether a candidate has developed sufficient intuition over the course of their training. I never saw the test in person before I took it and I never practiced for it. I only got one piece of advice from a fellow *sempai* immediately before I sat in front of Phillip Legare, Bujinkan Dai Shihan, who was giving me the test. The advice was, "When you close your eyes, go to your happy place. When it gets interrupted, let your body do what it already knows it needs to do." I sat with my back turned to

---

[13] Gavin de Becker wrote about intuition in *The Gift of Fear*.

the guy with the wooden sword, closed my eyes and thought about my family back home. The next thing I remember was being on the other side of the room, sōke yelling out, "OKEY!" and everyone around clapping. My intuition saved me.

Only after a few months did the moment of the test actually flash through my head again. Just before my body rolled away from the wooden sword, a sudden, strong, and uncomfortable feeling had taken over my entire body. This feeling catapulted my body nearly two meters away without any conscious intention.

Bob Proctor always says that when we pray, we talk to God. *Intuition*, he says, is when God talks back to us. In a way, intuition represents a connection of our mind to the world around us and helps us resolve many difficult situations by providing us answers out of thin air. Actually, it is not out of thin air. Many philosophers believed that the joint consciousness, where all information is stored, exists, that it is everywhere around us and that we are able to connect to it with our intuitive factor. Gavin de Becker mentions several examples of intuition in his book. He says that intuition provides us with the right information at the right time in order to protect us.

We all have intuition, the gift that serves to protect our own interests and wellbeing. We need to practice listening to it and not ignore or shush it because it doesn't seem logical. True intuition is always right and always has our best interest at heart.

These are your weapons. Choose which ones are more important to you at this point in your journey. Learn their basics, their purposes, and how to use them in your daily life. These faculties—these *weapons*—can hurt you if you don't use them properly. The wrong thinking will not give you a deadly stab or a broken arm, but it will give you anxiety, a lack of faith, stress, fear, or even disease. These are also serious injuries that can cripple our lives.

You can find many resources on each of these faculties. Remember what Earl Nightingale says: "Only a woman who decided to make a pie will search for a recipe." Decide which faculty you want to develop, and then go do it.

Every adversity, every failure, every heartache carries with it the seed of an equal or even greater benefit!

—**Napoleon Hill**

CHAPTER XI

Attitude

"While we are making plans, God is laughing at us."

This is a less famous Serbian proverb. It is teaching us that no matter how hard we plan, we cannot physically or mentally prepare for all the different scenarios in life: failing at a project, losing a job, divorcing, experiencing war, experiencing pandemics—you name it. It is impossible to predict what will life bring us from one moment to the next. The question is, how should we treat the things that matter to us when from one day to the next something might happen that will slow us down or stop us? How do we deal with our vision knowing that change is the only constant thing in this world?

In the dojo, we teach beginners to be aware of their body, then to focus on technique, and then to pay attention to their feeling while executing the *kata*. We use a principle called *Shin Gi Tai Ichi*, or *spirit, technique, body (should be) one*. This is a very simple translation. Please be aware that Japanese expressions have different meanings depending on the context or level of understanding. The purpose of this book is not to bring you deep into the art itself (I am definitely not the one to do that—there are many martial artists better equipped to do so) but to demonstrate how even basic principles from the west can also be found in the east; there are many ways to speak one truth. Also, in order to understand the various layers of these expressions you probably have to spend some years studying language and art. (I apologize to all martial artists and those who speak Japanese for my basic and somewhat laic interpretation of certain expressions.) Moreover, if you really want to understand the depth of these expressions, go to the training. One can only truly understand these things only through practice.

The best way to spot this composition of the three is through *kamae*, or posture. We learn different postures in order to execute different techniques. Whenever we talk about kamae, we try to explain to beginners that it is not only about body positioning but also about positioning of the mind and heart (spirit). Only then you have the right kamae.

What we call kamae in martial arts training we refer to as *attitude* in the world of coaching. Here, we define attitude as the composition of your thoughts, feelings, and actions, where all three need to be aligned as one. The composition of all three ingredients is what makes attitude. The correct alignment of these components is crucial for the process of growth. If you think one, feel another, and execute something completely different … this is a true recipe for disaster. Proper kamae is one of the main factors contributing to successful technique. Proper attitude is one of the main factors contributing to individual success![14]

The question becomes what is the proper attitude especially towards uncertainty or challenge? When practicing martial

---

[14] You can listen about attitude in "The Magic Word" audio from Earl Nightingale.

arts, we try to simulate many different situations. We practice our kamae (attitude) in defense, in offense, etc. This is our safe space where we can practice so that we are able to survive when necessary. Of course, unexpected things happen while sparring, but our time in the dojo is like a simulation preparing us for real-world situations. If you find yourself in a problem with someone on the street, they're not going to wait for you to warm up or to slip on your good running shoes and comfortable pants. When bad things happen, we are usually unprepared for them—they come as a surprise.

Business is very similar: Your product testing results come in bad when you're about to go to market; you just realized someone has copied your idea before you completed it and they are now selling it all around; a client that you desperately needed in order to make ends meet cancelled on you ten minutes before the meeting. Change is everywhere. Unexpected things happen daily.

In training, we practice so that we can face unexpected scenarios. When the technique says you should stop someone from pulling their sword, but they beat you to it, you have to change what you were intending to do and continue with your movement. You cannot do the technique you were intending to do because your opponent moved the wrong foot, you need to change to a different technique. Please understand, we do not practice so that we may know every different scenario—it is practically impossible! What we do is develop our *attitude* towards the idea of change.

This principle we practice in Bujinkan is called *Banpen Fugyō*. The basic translation of this expression is: *ten thousand (or infinite) changes, no surprise*. The deeper meaning is: *to face uncertainty without surprise or fear*. How can we achieve this? The first and most important thing is to not fight the change. This can take a lot of our energy. Because the change is usually something outside of our control, it can be useless. The three steps to facing the change are to accept, to adapt, and to keep going.

Accept: Denial in training can get you seriously hurt. You cannot deny that the punch is coming. You have to accept the situation. Accepting the change doesn't mean surrendering, it means refocusing away from what you cannot influence (the external situation) towards what you can influence (yourself). I used to suffer from severe anxiety. Once, I experienced a full-blown panic attack during a long flight. Anyone with experience will tell you that panic attacks are horrible—but it's the *fear* of panic attacks that is crippling! With time, I learned that mentally accepting that the panic attack was coming gave me a certain power over the fear. Telling myself that I know exactly what is happening with my body provided me with relief. With time, my anxiety subsided completely.

Adapt: The initial plan can be adapted to work with the new reality. You wanted to perform one technique, but you can change to another. The idea is to have the desired result and not to insist on achieving it by performing one specific movement. Many times, the initial negative momentum can be redirected to benefit us if we manage to adapt. Someone grabbed you in training even if you tried to prevent it—great! The fact they grabbed you now means that hand is not available to them anymore. Adapting can give you a huge advantage if you use the momentum.

Keep moving: The most important step when the opponent is attacking is for you to keep moving. In life, whatever happens, you need to keep moving towards the goal. Wanting to shift our deep system of beliefs represents a huge change for both parts of our mind. Our thinking mind can welcome the change, but our emotional mind (the subconscious) interprets any change as a threat to the status quo. Our subconscious *loves* the status quo; it will fight any paradigm shift we impose on it for as long as it can even though change itself can be very good for us! This is why it is vitally important to keep doing the daily things that bring us closer to our goal despite the challenges that we will face.

Nine out of ten people that I coach or mentor, within the first two weeks of their lessons, experience a crisis that prevents them from fulfilling the tasks related to the goal they have set. I know to anticipate this, and I know that only through an attitude of *banpen fugyō* can I help to lead them out of their crisis. It is not a question of whether you will face the storm on the road to your vision, it is a question of how soon you will face it. This is why developing a good attitude is important—infinite changes, no surprises.

The only thing that is constant in the world is change. And the only thing we can and should work on is how we position ourselves towards this change. Accept, adapt, and keep going. Even if you disregard every principle in this book and only work on developing a great attitude your results will soon show how significant it really is.

Your vision and consequent goal will require developing a great alignment of thoughts, feelings, and actions. It is not about *wanting* something, it is about *expecting* it and performing each day in a way that affirms your expectations regardless of the obstacles along the way. This is the right attitude. While you are making your plans, God might be laughing. But maybe God is laughing because he has an even better plan for you.

> Everything can be taken from a man but one thing: the last of human freedoms – to choose one's attitude in any given set of circumstances, to choose one's own way.
>
> —**Viktor Frankl**

CHAPTER XII

Vital Points

This woman has every right in the world to be angry about life and destiny, but Pam is out there right now helping others to grow and live happier lives.

Do you like going to the dentist? Why not? Is it the *fear* of pain, or is it the pain itself? I can remember how, when I was still practicing dentistry, my patients reacted differently to pain depending on whether the pain was mixed with fear or not. In medical school you learn that pain is a combination of objective impulses and a subjective interpretation of those impulses. In a dental chair you can really experience how people who fear visiting the dentist are highly sensitive to pain and pressure stimuli.

As an individual in martial arts I have learned that inflicting pain and receiving pain are normal parts of the learning process. When you have a new person in the dojo, they need to receive slight punches in order to learn about pain and the way their body (and mind) react to it. The purpose of this is never to hurt them. (Side note: if you ever go to any school of martial arts and people are being seriously injured on daily basis, please leave.) This can happen, and I did have my share of injuries, but it should be a rare occurrence.

Experiencing pain in training is the standard way to learn and grow. First, you learn how your body reacts to pain whether by falling, moving, being hit, etc. Second, you learn to deal with the pain without having your mind fully consumed by it. When you are on the ground and someone has their knee pinned on the inner part of your thigh, it is easy to get lost in the pain and be overwhelmed by emotion.

It's not that different in life. You must learn how to not get lost in the pain, and you have to keep moving. As a small child you fall, bang your head, cry, bleed—that is a standard way of learning how to walk (and how to fall properly). Yet no child ever stays on the ground. They get back up and keep moving.

In training we learn about pain through *kyūsho*. These are specific pressure points on the human body that send pain and other signals to the brain when they are stimulated. We also refer to them as vital points. In our martial arts there are many vital points that we learn during training (around 200) but we usually focus on the most common ones. Stimulation of these points might lead to a withdraw reflex which makes body move away from the source of pain. One might feel sick in the head, feel a loss of energy, or in more extreme cases, experience unconsciousness or possibly even death.

When I was attending a seminar with two Spanish dai shihans, one of them was also a practitioner of *Amatsu Tatara*, a healing art of pressing kyūsho (pressure points) to restore the body's energy and even heal sickness. As a side note, many other types of massage can stimulate these points with healing in mind. Interestingly, this sensei was the first one to point out to me that depending on how you are pressing the vital points you can either inflict pain or stimulate healing. The difference is in the direction you press. Imagine this: pressing with different motions on the same point of your body can either cause healing or cause death. If you transfer this to life, this is how our ability to direct pain plays a vital role.

Pain exists in our daily life. However, depending on how we take it, we can end up with different results from experiencing the same sensation. Pain can cause suffering to the point where we want to just crawl back in our bed and lose the will to live. It can also be the source of our biggest moments of healing. It is not about the sensation itself, but rather, it is about where we direct it. There are people who experience enormous amounts of pain who come back from it stronger and more healed than ever before. This strong sensation that is usually caused by heartbreaking life events is, ironically, responsible for creating some of the greatest books, songs, life altering projects—you name it.

I believe there is no greater pain than seeing your child leave this planet before you. It was October 2018, and I noticed a new blog by *New York Times* bestselling author, Pam Grout. I consider Pam a friend given that we stayed in touch years after her first workshop in Bern in February 2015. She is, by any standard, a remarkable human full of love and gratefulness. And on that cold day in October, I read in her blog that she had lost her only child, Taz, an amazing twenty-five-year-old girl. She had an aneurism and died within minutes of collapsing. There was no warning or signal; she was perfectly healthy. Suddenly, she was just gone.

I believe that, on any scale of pain, it could not get worse than this. Only a person who has lost a child can understand this pain. I am sure that there were moments where Pam wanted to just give up. Everyone would! But Pam did the unthinkable! She continued her practice of gratefulness being thankful for all the years she had the gift of being with her loving daughter. She was thankful that she had the opportunity to be a mother to a child like Taz for twenty-five full years. Pam started the Taz 222 foundation to help others who are going through life struggles. Every year on February 22nd, Pam donates financial help to people who need it. This woman has every right in the world to be angry about life and destiny, but Pam is out there right now helping others to grow and live happier lives.

The thing I learned from this remarkable woman is that the only known antidote to pain and suffering is gratitude. When we are grateful, we don't have space in our heart for emotions such as fear, anxiety, depression, etc. When focusing on the things we are grateful for, new things that we appreciate begin to emerge. Gratitude itself has several important levels of depth.

The first level is being able to list everything we are thankful for; this represents our ability to be aware and remember things that we are blessed with. That is a good start. The second level is that we are able to imagine what our life would be like without the things we give thanks for. The final level of gratitude is giving back. Being generous to others because you feel that life is generous to you. Every time I have a bad day and things are looking gloomy, I go out and do an act of kindness; putting chocolate in my neighbor's mailbox, buying something for the person I care about, or helping a complete stranger.

If you want to cultivate the attitude of gratitude, I recommend practicing all three levels. They provide remarkable results. In the end, I also recommend reading *Thank & Grow Rich* by Pam Grout. If there is one person to learn from about this topic it is absolutely Pam.

He is a wise man who does not grieve for the things
which he has not, but rejoices for those which he has.

—Epictetus (55 - 135) Greek philosopher

The Final Chapter
- Immovable Spirit

"What I find funny about that type of person is that today he works behind my back, but tomorrow, it could be anyone else's back—maybe even yours."

Early on, people would often ask me if I was really willing to get bruised a few times each week just because there was a vague possibility that one day someone might attack me on the street. They didn't understand how much practicing martial arts really develops human potential. It was the same with coaching. People don't often have a clear idea of why someone would need a coach. They tend to think coaching is about motivation or giving advice. Someone who is really a specialist in human development helps others evolve on every level using nothing but the client's own potential in order to achieve incredible results.

A client once told me a story that demonstrates how working on yourself and your goals daily can benefit you on a larger scale. Let's be honest—sometimes you can work for days, weeks, and months without visible change. And then, with one right thought at the right time, clear of any fear, worry, or doubt, the true power of self and the change that has taken place will reveal itself.

This client was having dinner with her manager and some colleagues. During the conversation, the manager teased her that someone in the company had his eye on her position and was working behind her back to get it. The manager was expecting a reaction from my client; he was expecting her to show fear or, at the very least, demonstrate that she would do everything required to keep her position.

I know the type. This manager was the kind of person who likes to test people. He enjoyed controlling them by making them anxious and fearful. You won't believe how many people like this are in leading positions of major corporations. She told me that she stayed silent at first then smiled lightly and responded with a perfectly steady voice: "What I find funny about that type of person is that today he works behind my back, but tomorrow, it could be anyone else's back—maybe even yours." She continued eating as if nothing happened. Once he heard this, the manager was silent for a few moments. No one talked. Then, the manager stood up from the table and walked outside. At the time, she didn't understand what was going on. Later, she found out that the manager walked outside and instantly made a phone call to that same colleague with a clear statement that nobody in the company was allowed to work behind other people's backs.

Just imagine, if she had reacted instead by worrying about this situation it would reflect on her feelings, her behavior, and eventually her results. There was a real chance this might have cost her the job in the end. Events in life don't just happen randomly. Many times they are the result of a long process that starts with a thought involving worry, fear, stress, and anxiety.

Today more than ever, we are reactive beings. We are very easily disturbed, upset, angry, frustrated, and insecure. This usually comes as a result of things that happen on the outside; they drive our behavior, and consequently, our results. Once we allow the outside to drive our behavior, it is really difficult to achieve inner balance. Why is this happening? We want to have certain control over what happens in our lives. It is human and it is normal. Usually, we believe the way to do this is by controlling the outside. When that fails (and it always does because no one can control the outside world) we become upset, insecure, and full of fear.

Imagine an ocean. On the surface of the ocean there are waves that are breaking and hitting the shore. They are governed by the moon and it is impossible to control them. Under the waves and the constant movement there is a deep, peaceful sea where the waters are still. Life resides in the depths of ocean that is not dependent on the sun or the moon—not dependent on outside circumstances. Our lives are similar, crashing waves on the surface; but if we go a bit under the surface, we will discover the depths of the eternal calm.

Imagine a person who stays calm during a storm; a person who does not even blink when someone is yelling at them. Imagine developing yourself to the extent that you can perfectly and naturally respond to any situation rather than reacting. Instead of letting your fears control your reaction, you remain unshaken. Responding comes from perfect stillness where we are allowed to think clearly without letting emotions interfere. Reacting always comes from the emotional mind and is governed by our paradigm.

This principle is also common in martial arts. It is a goal of advanced martial artists to achieve *mushin*.[15] The character *shin* can

---

[15] Dai Shihan Arnaud Cousergue perfectly explains *mushin* in his blog https://kumablog.org

mean *heart, mind, spirit,* or *inner strength.* Mushin is translated as *no spirit* or *empty mind.* One can achieve mushin when one's mind is free from thoughts of anger and fear, and free of one's ego. There is no thought or judgment, so you are free to respond towards anything and anyone without hesitation or disturbance.

In martial arts, it is believed that mushin is the sixth element. It is a sort of consciousness where natural movement becomes truly free to be expressed. This is vitally important because achieving peace on the inside causes a perfect response on the outside. This is an example of natural balance.

This is why, without a doubt, everyone who has ever been successful in anything claims that you have to be the master of your thoughts. One of the greatest powers in mastering your thoughts is mastering the calmness of your mind.

> "The calm man, having learned how to govern himself, knows how to adapt himself to others; and they, in turn, reverence his spiritual strength, and feel that they can learn from him and rely upon him. The more tranquil a man becomes, the greater is his success, his influence, his power for good."[16]

The immovable spirit represents great power. It doesn't matter whether you are a martial artist, the CEO of multimillion-dollar company, or a barista at Starbucks. We can all use this universal power to stay calm so outside winds cannot shake us.

Mastering mushin requires a certain amount of time spent alone in meditation, contemplation, or guided solitude. It requires zooming out of any current situation that is making

---

[16] James Allen wrote the chapter "Serenity" in his famous book *As a Man Thinketh.*

you anxious and observing today as one tiny piece of the huge puzzle that is your life. By practicing calmness of mind we tap into a greater knowledge of the eternal calm. Letting go of both our inner demons and our outer disturbances will eventually lead to mastering our own life. This is the calmness of mind. This is the state where our response is natural and free from any form of anger, worry, fear, or other emotions. It is free from any technique or form. It is perfect because it is clear, effortless, and natural.

The reply that my client gave at that dinner with her manager was truly the result of long and patient effort in self-control. Less than a year after that dinner, her manager left the company and she received a salary increase and promotion. She finally understood the power of the immovable spirit and the active role it plays in our own process of becoming.

> Calmness of mind is one of the beautiful jewels of wisdom. It is the result of long and patient effort in self-control. Its presence is an indication of ripened experience, and of a more than ordinary knowledge of the laws and operations of thought.
>
> **—James Allen**

In the End

We are all self-made, but only the successful will admit it.

—Earl Nightingale

In the many years I lived abroad, I spent more time by myself than many people spend alone in their lifetime. I would finish university class or work and wander down the streets for hours. During this time, I failed at relationships, I failed at work, and I failed at some of my personal projects. But at the same time, I finished university, found a great job, started my own business, rediscovered myself emotionally, faced some of my greatest fears, and emerged on the other side (talk about failure being an integral part of success).

I remember only two types of these long walks. One was walking and thinking about my current circumstances and where to go from there, thinking from one day to another. I would walk and feel every tiny stone on the path. Every step was heavier than the previous one. In those moments, I felt completely lost and alone.

Then there was another type of walk. As I walked, I thought about my vision, imagining how it would feel if it became a reality. Those walks I could go on for hours. I was full of energy and I could see myself somewhere else despite what was actually going on inside or outside of me. If you ask me today which type of walk I prefer, I think you could easily guess the correct one. It does not matter what kind of failure I was experiencing; if my focus was on my vision, I was happy regardless of what was currently happening.

We can speak of principles of self-mastery all day long, but we have to be clear about one thing: self-mastery only comes through purposeful work. Having a clear vision and a well-defined goal is the first pre-requisite for achieving self-mastery. Only when the vision is there can you start working on different challenges, especially the paradigms and your self-image, because your own experience and deep-seated beliefs will control how far you can go. Your job is to break through the old beliefs and replace them with new ones. This is the only way to get new results.

In the beginning, you need to work hard; later, you need to learn to work smart. When I passed my *godan* test and asked what I should study next, Sōke of Shinden Fudo Ryu Nagato sensei told me: "Until 4th dan, you need blood, sweat, and tears. After *sakki* test, no strength, no power in your training. Do not try to win, but remember—you can't lose." I interpreted this as a message telling me to stop trying to win battles for my ego. Instead, I should be perseverant on my road and never give up because the person who never gives up eventually ends up winning.

All the different sources I have studied on the topics of self-defense and self-development, in the end, revolve around answering the three questions. Where are you going? Where are you now? Who are you, truly? There is no universal one-size-fits-all answer for everyone; there is a certain roadmap we need to follow and answers we need to discover through daily work. This is what I always try to provide to my students, colleagues, clients, and friends, and what I tried to provide to you in this book.

You might already know your goal, but you need to work on self-image. Or, maybe the old paradigms are the issue. Focus on your own needs. If you don't know where to begin, start with charting your values, vision, and goals. Be willing to experience temporary defeat. Create the space for your vision, change your non-productive habits, forget controlling anything other than yourself, and welcome any experience along your road. Work on your self-image and mental faculties, have the right attitude, practice gratitude and persevere on your road. In this process it is not important how many hours you spend studying and practicing in a day; what's important is that you actually do it every single day.

And please remember to have fun! Life will occasionally slap you on the face, but this is not an invitation to go through the life with both hands over your head. Make sure to nurture your playful heart. No beauty in life can be experienced with a constant fear of the life itself.

The true meaning of being a *beginner with the black* belt is that you are on the road to your own self-mastery. Your vision is your black belt. Look at yourself in the mirror and understand who you need to become today so that you might reach your destination tomorrow. It really doesn't matter where you are now. Wherever you are, this is your new beginning. So do yourself two favors: start moving today, and keep enjoying the road. Those are the true Principles of Heaven, Earth, and Human. And that is what I wish for you.

Ninjutsu Poem

My parents are the Heaven and earth.
My home is my body.
My power is my loyalty.
My magic is my training.
My life and my death is breathing.
My body is control.
My eyes are the sun and the moon.
My ears are sensitivity.
My laws are self-protection.
My strength is adaptability.
My ambition is taking every opportunity with fullness.
My friend is my mind.
My enemy is carelessness.
My protection is right action.
My weapons are everything that exists.
My strategy is one foot in front of the other.
My way is Ninjutsu.

(unknown Author)

Sources Mentioned in the Book and Further Recommendations

Here are some books and sources that I mention in the book.

Self-Development

Think & Grow Rich – Napoleon Hill

Psycho-Cybernetics – Dr. Maxwell Maltz

As a Man Thinketh – James Allen

The Gift of Fear – Gavin de Becker

Thank & Grow Rich – Pam Grout

Man's Search for Meaning – Dr. Viktor Frankl

The Science of Getting Rich – Wallace D. Wattles

Born Rich – Bob Proctor

No Excuses – Brian Tracy

Martial Arts

Ethical Warrior – Jack Hoban

Essence of Ninjutsu – Dr. Masaaki Hatsumi

Ninja: Ancient Shadow Warriors of Japan (The Secret History of Ninjutsu) – Dr. Kacem Zoughari

The Essence of Budo: The Secret Teachings of the Grandmaster – Dr. Masaaki Hatsumi

Life Secrets of the Amatsu Tatara – Peter King

Articles & Blogs

"The Common Denominator of Success" – Albert E. N. Gray

Explanations on Sakizuke, by Dai Shihan Duncan Stewart: https://tazziedevil.wordpress.com/2012/06/13/thoughts-on-rank

Explanations on Mushin by Dai Shihan Arnaud Cousergue: https://kumablog.org/2014/07/07/mushin-no-intention

Audio & Video Programs

Magic in Your Mind – Mary Morrissey & Bob Proctor

The Strangest Secret – Earl Nightingale

The Magic Word – Earl Nightingale

You Were Born Rich – Bob Proctor & John Kanary

Coaching Programs

Thinking into Results – Bob Proctor & Sandy Gallagher

Lead the Field – Bob Proctor & Sandy Gallagher

If you would like to practice Bujinkan, I recommend you find the closest dojo and try it. You will love it. Gambatte!

Next to her profession in healthcare, Ana has been coaching both individuals and groups for several years now and facilitating programs by the Proctor Gallagher Institute that transformed her life as well as the lives of her clients. If you are interested in finding out more about the coaching programs that Ana is facilitating, please contact her on following pages:

Website: anastevanovic.com

Email: ance018@gmail.com

Facebook: https://www.facebook.com/ana.stevanovic

LinkedIn: www.linkedin.com/in/ana-stevanović-DMD

About the Author

A na Stevanović DMD, MSc, was born in Niš, Serbia. She graduated in dentistry from the Faculty of Medicine at the University of Niš, and was active as President of the European Dental Students' Association during her time as a student. After spending several years in the dental office, Ana was awarded a scholarship to join the Master's in Healthcare Management, Economics and Policy (MIHMEP) program in SDA, Bocconi, Milan, Italy. Upon graduating, she moved to Luzern, Switzerland, where she lives and works as Head of Professional Education at Curaden AG, a Swiss oral care company. Her passion for education and human development led her to become a certified Proctor Gallagher Institute consultant in 2018, and she has been coaching individuals and groups ever since. Ana has been a practitioner of Japanese martial arts since her high school days (she currently practices at Bujinkan Buyu Dojo in Zürich), and is currently ranked 7th Dan in Bujinkan.

HEARTS to be HEARD

Giving a Voice to Creativity!

With every donation, a voice will be given to
the creativity that lies within the hearts of
our children living with diverse challenges.

By making this difference, children that may
not have been given the opportunity to have their
Heart Heard will have the freedom to create
beautiful works of art and musical creations.

Donate by visiting

HeartstobeHeard.com

We thank you.